M000032240

# A Special Note from the Publisher

These stories of how an obsession with fly fishing has affected—for better or worse—his or her romantic relationships are true. In certain instances, names have been changed or situations slightly masked to protect the innocent from embarrassment and the publisher from the guilty and their junkyard-dog lawyers. You know who you are. As I have instructed the hangman to chisel on my modest slab of New England granite: YOU CAN'T INVENT THIS STUFF.

# Till Death or Fly Fishing Do Us Part

*When Your Passion Collides with Hers,*
*Can the Relationship Be Far Behind?*

## By Thomas R. Pero

*With a Cast of Addicted Anglers and*
*Fishing Widows*

Illustrations by Whitney Martin

"Sometimes I wonder if men and women really suit each other. Perhaps they should live next door and just visit now and then."
— Katherine Hepburn


"Fly-fishing is such great fun, I have often felt, that it really ought to be done in bed. Not that high frolic is the only thing the pursuit of fish and the pursuit of females have in common; these ancient sports have more going for them—as I'll now try to tell why."
— Robert Traver

*Library of Congress Cataloging-in-Publication Data*
Pero, Thomas R.
Till Death or Fly Fishing Do Us Part./Thomas R. Pero et al.—1st ed.
    p. cm.
ISBN 9780974642789
Fly fishing. 2. Wit and humor. I. Title.

Library of Congress Control Number  2008934106

Book and cover design by John Cole Graphic Design
Illustrations by Whitney Martin © 2005 – 2008
Published by Wild River Press, Post Office Box 13360,
Mill Creek, Washington 98082 USA
Wild River Press Web site address: www.wildriverpress.com
Printed in the United States of America

10  9  8  7  6  5  4  3  2  1

# Contents

# Confessions of a Fishing Widow

By Jennifer Axtell

SEVENTEEN YEARS AGO WHEN I FIRST MET Nathaniel, my husband-to-be, Than was a teenaged life guard at my neighborhood pool, a beanpole with a strange arm-and-neck tan. I knew he was a fisherman because he had tacked some photographs of big bass he had caught on the pool bulletin board. I remember one batch very well—in one picture, he held up a ruler alongside an oversized fish; in another, he held the same ruler beside his bulging crotch, into which he'd stuffed a cucumber or something.

I knew right then that he was weird, but I had no real idea just how serious his affliction was.

Seven moves, six graduations, 30-plus fly rods and one child later, we're still together, though I sometimes wonder what would have happened if I'd stayed in Virginia and married a normal person—an insurance salesman, say, or a chiropractor. Instead, I married a fishing guide, writer and obsessive freak who spends as much time yapping about flies and rivers and trout and bass as he does actually fishing for them. And, believe me, that's a lot of yapping.

There are days in the spring and summer months—peak guiding season—when we say, "Good morning," followed by "Good night," with not much else in between. And there have been times I've come really, really close to piling all the fly rods, chicken necks and fishing books in the front yard and torching them. But from the start I knew what I was getting into.

\* \* \*

OUR FIRST REAL DATE (I WON'T COUNT THE Arby's Kids Meal dinner) was an unmemorable movie. Our second "date" was a trip to Shenandoah National Park, where he forced me to slog across hill and through dale in search of some brook trout stream he had only a vague idea how to find. Several wrong turns and miles later, we found it, and Than climbed down into a small gorge and started creeping upstream like an Army sniper. I took some pictures, then sat on a lumpy rock and read.

That night we set up a tent Than had borrowed from his dad. In his zeal to cut "unnecessary weight" (two extra fly rods, fully loaded vest, etc., did not qualify), he'd left the rain fly at home. Of course, right after dark, a huge thunderstorm blew in and dumped an inch of cold rain on us, soaking our sleeping bags and everything else. The next morning I awoke shivering in a puddle, only to find Than snoozing comfortably in his chest waders.

I should have run for the car and never looked back; instead, we got engaged.

\* \* \*

IT WAS A WARM AUTUMN DAY IN 1993 AND THAN wanted to throw poppers for bass in a private lake down the road from his folks' house. His bassing forays normally involved my helping him drag his aluminum johnboat through woods, across several deep ravines, to a secluded cove where the owners of the lake couldn't see us fishing. This particular day I resisted but he made a larger-than-usual scene and said we would only be dock fishing. I relented. At the dock, he asked me to open up his bass box and hand him something out of it. I should have known something was up—he never let me touch his gear. I did as he asked. There, in the middle of all that deer hair, was a diamond ring.

"Will you marry me?" he asked, still swishing line over his head. Again, I should have disappeared, but he looked so cute in his BASS ASSASSIN T-shirt and cut-offs, and the ring was really nice. So I said, "Yes."

*Damned diamonds.*

Bass were one thing, but then we moved from Virginia to western North Carolina so he could be closer to the trout streams he grew up fishing as a boy. He wasn't guiding then, but he worked at a newspaper until late into the night so he could devote Wednesdays (a comp day), Saturdays and Sundays to trout. I went along on the weekends, only because we lived in the boondocks and there wasn't much else to do there except shuck corn and count our neighbors' missing teeth. I had found a part-time job teaching mentally disabled adults, which meant now my entire week was devoted to the developmentally challenged. Eventually, we moved south to Brevard, so I could take a better teaching job, and to put Than closer to his beloved Davidson River.

Than started guiding part time, then full time, then all the time. In retrospect, I thought it would be good because he would get more "river time," as he calls it, and spend less time away from home chasing slimy things with scales. Plus, he'd get paid. But I quickly learned that for every day spent on the river with some Florida tourist, it takes two days of "personal fishing" to "scout the best holes" and "keep on top of the hatches."

Yeah, *right.*

Then there are the hours and hours he spends hunched over his tying desk, or on the phone with fishing buddies, or reading books or magazine articles. Trout now consume our lives, his by choice and mine by proxy. We have a rainbow trout telephone, trout artwork, fiberglass trout replicas, trout posters, trout calendars, trout dishware, even a beer bottle collection featuring—you guessed it —trout.

Even our two-year-old son, Clark, can't escape the pervasive aura. Among his first words were "reel," "rod," "boat" and "wah-wah." He can't count above 10 yet but he can differentiate between a largemouth and a brookie. He can cast his miniature bamboo rod with aplomb and net Papa's fish like a guide-in-training. That's not a shock to me, considering that Clark probably floated more rivers In Utero than most adults do in a lifetime.

When I was five months pregnant, Than dragged me out to oxygen-deprived Telluride, Colorado, for a bluegrass festival and fishing on the San Miguel, then down to the San Juan in New Mexico for an all-day float trip in scorching temperatures. I drank lots of water and felt pretty good, until the following day when he insisted on wading the upper flats for six hours while I read in the truck parked in the shade.

The temperature climbed to 105° Fahrenheit—I had to run the motor so I could sit in air conditioning. Then the truck ran out of gas, so I persuaded a local fishing guide to run me up to Abe's for refueling. By the time I got back, Than was sitting on the curb with that shit-eating grin he gets after he "tore 'em up." That day I almost tore *him* up.

\* \* \*

YEARS AGO, WHEN WE FIRST STARTED TALKING about having kids, Than (only half-jokingly) said he wanted to have a boy and name him "Trout." (It seems people with strange names want to inflict the same misery on their own offspring.) I told him, sure, as long as he paid me $5,000 on the day of delivery. Needless to say, that kind of cash was more likely to be stashed away for a trip to Alaska or Montana, so I was pretty safe making such a deal.

Sure enough: A couple of months after Clark was born, Than flew to Katami National Park for nine days as the host of a group of anglers from Davidson River Outfitters. I was on maternity leave, so it didn't bother me, but our parents and friends thought he was nuts to leave us. I didn't hear from him for a week, and wondered whether grizzly bears might leave me a single mom. But I kept reminding myself that if anybody got eaten streamside, it would likely be someone with more meat on his bones than my lanky husband.

Why have I stuck with him all these years, enduring spousal neglect and interminable fishing outings? Because I love him. Because when the fishing is good or when his clients have done well, he is much more fun to be around than when he was stressed out from deadlines and meetings.

There are some pluses to being married to a trout bum. The guiding business gives him the flexibility to keep Clark twice a week, and even more in the off-season, which is good for their relationship and our family. I don't fish myself, so I don't understand the all-consuming nature of it, but I do know that I have visited some beautiful places thanks to Than's obsession—the Rockies, the Pacific Northwest, the northern Appalachians, the Ozarks among them. Than likes to say, "Trout don't live in ugly places," and I can vouch for that.

Do I like the fact that we have four boats clogging up the yard? No. But I like floating the French Broad River on a sunny day. Do I get embarrassed when he climbs atop our car at the Texaco station to snatch some bug that's drawn to the lights? Yes, but I'd rather he get excited about the mating ritual of a mayfly than Internet porn. Marriage is about compromise, and good ones achieve a certain balance. For every trip to Labrador for trophy brook trout, there must be a family week at the beach. For every new reel, there'd better be some sapphire earrings. As long as the gutters get cleaned occasionally, I don't care if he goes fishing on his days off.

But don't tell him I said so.

## Note on the Author

Jennifer Axtell of Bevard, North Carolina, is thrilled that her husband, trout bum Nathaniel Axtell, now reports to an actual job managing Headwater Outfitters. She is a school librarian.

# The Enabler   By Rob Lewis

TO MARRY SOMEONE WHO FISHES WOULD BE cool, I once thought, a fly-fishing fanatic's dream come true. My life has taken an interesting turn, however, now that I'm actually married to someone who is self-sufficient on the river. These days I'm not feeling so indispensable.

Kim took up fly fishing like a child who had just discovered ice cream. She is the kind of chick who can hang out around the campfire with my trout-bum friends and speak fluent river-rat lingo—right down to the twisted Latin pronunciation of the mayflies hatching that day, and their willingness to commit to either the emerger or the dun.

To some men this might sound like marrying the Carmen Electra of trout fishing, but I've gradually realized that now there are *two* of us afflicted, with no cure in sight.

There are differences in our approaches to the sport. There was a time when I had to stop and think about whether I really needed that new fly line; Kim refuses to use anything but top-of-the-line equipment. I am constantly reminded why vests are better than fanny packs, why mono is superior to fluoro, why a surgeon's knot is better than a clinch.

As I recall, she first contracted the illness when

she came to visit me while I was living in Montana. We fished every day, to the end. When we were about to reel in on the Henry's Fork, she *insisted* we stay, and then I landed the biggest rainbow trout I had ever hooked. That's one way to get a guy's attention.

Next, we spent the day of our rehearsal dinner chasing stripers off Long Island; in our wedding pictures we look like a pair of raccoons, sun-stained and wind-burned. Once again, she insisted we go. How could I resist? I was beginning to see a diabolical pattern developing—Kim was my enabler, and I hers.

After we finished packing the pickup with fly rod cases, our black dog, and a jumbo cooler of beer for the honeymoon drive to Florida to chase redfish for a week, a profound sense of being blissfully in love came over me. I tried to express what I was feeling. I'll never forget her reply: "We have a lifetime for fooling around. The red bite is on early so let's get some rest."

\* \* \*

OTHER THINGS HAVE CHANGED. AS PRIMARILY a production fly tier, I've noticed that I used to tie flies in lots of 25, 50, 100 pieces—now, when I re-count them to fill an order, there might be 21, 47 or 93, depending on how Kim likes the look of what I'm tying. I get my leaders in 10-piece boxes; when did they start putting only eight leaders in the box?

Following church, many families here in the Catskills spend Sundays traditionally carving ham or turkey around the dining-room table, anticipating the evening lineups on television. The river is our church. The night before, Kim picks up six-packs of cold Heineken and hard cider along with some pepperoni and something that looks like horse food. She meticulously organizes her tippets, hemostats and fly selections. Her admonition—"DON'T TOUCH MY SHIT!"—echoes in my ears like Hell's bells.

Walking the path to the river is like walking down the isle to the pew, even down to our Sunday best: Gore-Tex and the finest rolled graphite. I could swear I've seen Kim genuflect before she makes her first cast. Maybe she is praying for that 16-inch brown to rise to some booze-inspired pattern I con-cocted while she was fondling her tackle last night. More often than not her prayers are answered.

We were invited to Nantucket to try for the elusive dorado which occasionally show up to feast on baitballs. As my friend Milinko's boat idled out of the harbor, I summoned my testosterone-driven rules of engagement: "No pissing and moaning ... no 'I wanna go home.'" I was ready and well-rehearsed. Then reality set in. Those are some large waves out there. Our quick one-hour cruise turned into a two-and-a-half-hour dry-heave run for an episode of *Survivor*.

Kim proved particularly adept at marine multitasking: laughing at one of my friends while her 10-weight was bent severely as she managed in ladylike fashion to vomit discreetly out of the corner of her mouth. Yet she was still grinning from ear to ear. Not a knot was tied for her, not a fly chosen.

She was in charge of the rear-right gunwale and held it with authority. When the motor drive tangled the hydraulics and the lights went out on the way back in, all I remember is the sound of Kim's voice talking about not only the dozen dorado she took on the fly but also about how my male fly-fishing pals had to hide under the bow, and that cute shade of green they all displayed as if reflecting those beautiful migratory fish. One of the mates paid her his ultimate compliment: "That's one stone-cold, hardcore fishin' *bitch*."

Yes, she is.

\* \* \*

ONE SUMMER DAY, KIM AND I WERE SCOUTING for rising trout from Livingston Manor down through Roscoe along the Beaverkill as far west as Cooks Falls with only intermittent stops for a quick bite. We got 'em on every stage, from emerger to spinner. As early as it was in the game, we stopped riverside for a cold one and to watch the evening's festivities. Kim rubbed her hands together as though warming them for the next roll of the dice at the Bellagio.

We drove down to the Hazel Bridge to watch the river-worn old-school anglers casting dry flies on bamboo wands, speaking only amongst themselves as if the river and the trout were theirs and theirs alone. Little brown caddisflies bounced all over, dropping eggs everywhere. These true believers were casting upstream in unison, watching the current return their perfect dead-drifts. They were catching nothing.

Kim couldn't take it. She hopped out of the truck and waded in 150 yards downstream from the nearest angler. She was actually up under the bridge. With no instruction from me, she began

casting and shaking her rod erratically on the retrieve to mimic the naturally skittering bugs. She
hooked fish after fish. One by one the old coots
reeled in and left.

To my wife, Kim:

You are my soulmate and I'll love you till
death do us part, but it's time to talk and this is
the only way left to communicate with you. In
a fly-fishing and fly-tying family there can be
only one "Chosen One." Cleary that is you. Now
I need to stand up tall and tell you a few things.

1.  I can actually catch fish. I've resigned myself to the reality that I'll never again catch
more than you. All I ask is that you admit to
yourself that I was into all this before you entered my life.

2.  Do you remember whose waders you're
wearing? (Hint: They were mine.)

3.  I KNOW THE GODDAMN DIFFERENCE
BETWEEN 6X AND 7X TIPPET.

4.  Next year we go on my vacation to fish for
trout someplace weird. And not to a remote
Bahamian island so I can watch you lie in the
sun one day and then casually catch a dozen
four-pound bonefish the next.

5. As someone who guides for a good part of my living, why do I always feel like I owe *you* something after we fish together?
6. Can I have my 3-weight back?

\* \* \*

AS I WRITE THIS, OUR NINE-MONTH-OLD daughter, Kasey Montana Lewis, is sitting on my lap. Her mother is searching the Internet for a fly-fishing guide in Cabo San Lucas, for a much deserved spring break from work and baby, casting for roosterfish on the fly. I'm sure going to miss her.

### Note on the Author

Rob Lewis of Pound Ridge, New York is a full-time fly tier and fishing guide in the Catskills. His new waders are generously provided by his wife, Kim Lewis, who gets up early every morning and faithfully takes the commuter train into Manhattan, where she is an executive with Macy's.

# Search and Rescue   By Lucy Belter

IT WAS A LONG RIDE HOME.

It was five weeks before our wedding, and I had taken Rich, my fiancé, to a place I love: Acadia National Park and Mount Desert Island, Maine. I had imagined us walking and biking beautiful carriage paths around the coastal hills; hiking meticulously maintained, sub-arboreal forest trails; and enjoying the spectacular mountains-to-island-dotted ocean scenes in each other's company.

We did some of that.

As I was learning, however, Rich has to get a taste of fly fishing wherever he goes. He tried casting in the Atlantic Ocean at Sand Beach, the only sandy outlet in an otherwise craggy coastline. No fish, though. At the end of the last day of our extended weekend, just before departure, Rich wanted to try fishing in one more spot: Upper Hadlock Pond.

This kettle pond, fed by runoff from Bald Mountain, had a gnarly swamp at its north end. That's where we parked. "Twenty minutes," Rich said. I headed off to the woods to stretch my legs a bit before our long drive home to Massachusetts.

When I returned, he was nowhere in sight. I walked around the north perimeter of the pond until I could go no farther—still no view of Rich. I walked back to the car, scanned the rest of the pond from the road, and waited. No luck.

* * *

WITH MOUNTING ANXIOUS IMAGES OF RICH STUCK under a twisted tree or up to his neck in muck—and not yet knowing his exceptional resourcefulness in such situations—after waiting a full hour, I drove to a nearby country store. With fearful tears, I asked the shopkeeper to call in search and rescue, which she promptly did, all the while trying to reassure me.

By the time I arrived back at the parking spot, I could see flashing lights. Rich was standing there looking sheepish, with an ambulance and police car next to him. I thanked them and they left, but Rich and I were well onto the mainland part of the drive before we spoke. I was feeling sorely tested; he was feeling grateful that I had been so concerned.

And it was much, much later before Rich revealed to me that when the police had met up with him, "searching for a drowned fisherman," he had joined in the search until he figured out it was him they were looking for.

## Note on the Author

Lucy Belter of Georgetown, Massachusetts, is a massage therapy specialist. She lives with her husband, Rich Murphy, fly-tying wizard and author of *Fly Fishing for Striped Bass* (2007), winner of the Independent Publisher Silver Medal Award in the category of best sports and recreational book.

# Farewell, My Damp Departed Diva

By David L. Goodman

SHE WAS PRETTY AND BLONDE. SURELY MANY were prettier, maybe a few blonder; none lazier. She was a lanky Houston debutante with legs and loins as smooth as new running lines. She was also the gal who had everything. To shelter his line from "the violation of miscegenation and the other perils of the damnable thirteenth mendment [*sic*]," her great-great grandpapa—a vanquished Confederate general—had fled the rolling meadows of Virginia for the crusty scrub that would become his family's oil and gas bastion. Now the family's only worries were horizontal drilling of their fields by neighbors and matriculation into the Bayou Club by nobodies.

Our one year of marriage comprised a single season of salmon fishing on the Moisie and Restigouche rivers in Canada, then beats of the Gaula, Orkla, Namsen and Laerdal in Norway. As our protracted Norwegian fishing was about to end, a rare offer came to fish the Alta. When I invited my bride, she imploded in tears which my fishing companion, Bo Ivanovic, a more seasoned salmonist and husband, interpreted as "probably not an unqualified endorsement."

I happily introduced her to steelhead fishing on the Skagit, Squamish and Thompson rivers on the West Coast. I gave her Thanksgiving on a sewage-treatment effluent ditch in Kokomo, Indiana, that a bleached and buffed Midwestern steelhead guide driving a Dodge van full of filthy cats warranted as a "spring creek chock-a-block with steelhead." I treated her to midnight dry-fly fishing for channel cats on the Susquehanna; sight-fishing for giant tarpon on the Homosassa flats; billfishing in Quepos; bluefishing in Duck; several dozen days of trout fishing on the Beaverkill and Yellow Breeches —all connected by days on Pulaski's Salmon River, where the season is as endless as the species of fish and fishers.

She was a damp diva wrapped in wet neoprene.

\* \* \*

THE NIGHT THAT BEGAN THE SECOND YEAR OF our marriage, she said "Sweetheart, instead of coming to Norway tomorrow I've decided to go to a ladies' spa. I'll meet you in Maine when you return and we can drive up to your river together." After 18 months of conjugal bliss, including 12 idyllic months of marriage, I was disappointed though not alarmed that she would prefer the Golden Door to round-the-clock casting under the midnight sun. While the Norwegians call it the midnight sun because the northern sky is never dark around midsummer, they complain that they can go a generation or two without actually seeing the sun through the summer's clouds.

On our honeymoon the year before, we had 23 consecutive days when the rain stopped only to make way for hail and force-8 gale. My feelings were not the least bit hurt. Her aberrant decision was not a suggestion that she didn't appreciate the devotion I had lavished by letting her come on all these fishing trips. Obviously, it was a textbook symptom of the blackfly fever she had contracted the week before on the Moisie, where the flying scourge took advantage of the unexpectedly warm opening day to open their own season. She had looked so pathetic, the brushbottle flower-soft skin of her angular face, framed by her luminescence of unassistedly golden, almost etiolated hair, left grotesquely swollen and lopsided by the swarms of north woods blackflies that had savaged her. Besides, I knew her anxiety level rose exponentially the farther she got from Neiman Marcus.

I was not responsible. I had advised in the strongest terms against her wearing Joy or staying too long past dusk, when I gave her detailed directions with the compass and geodetic survey map and sent her on her way to the camp dump to watch the black bears frolic, while I went on my way to the evening bite to finally hook the "beau beau" 30-pounder I had risen 11 times during the morning session to the wild, canoe-shaking delight of the bowman who kept bellowing, "*le saumon s'amuse!*"

A Houston deb's habits die hard. The camp manager told me that when she came screaming back from the dump, he scrambled for his .30-06 until he saw in the million candlelights of his q-beam that she was fleeing not an enraged black bear sow but "half the blackflies on the North Shore."

Unfortunately, her blackfly-induced irrational behavior didn't subside before my SAS flight left Dulles, so I kissed her gently on a spot the blackflies hadn't assaulted and agreed I would pick her up in three weeks at the Presque Isle airport, for a gentle week fishing the Restigouche with one of the world's greatest gentlemen and tarpon fishermen, Billy Pate, and his then-newest if not favorite wife.

\* \* \*

THE FISHING IN NORWAY WAS TERRIBLE. HIGH water had left the gillies' huts bobbing in the fjord. My fishing mentor, Göran Andersson, the Newton of fly fishing, so magical with a fly rod they call him "Trollman" in his native Sweden, accepted a last-minute invitation to fish the rod my wife had whimsically abandoned. We spent two weeks martini-shaker cold, wet and fishless. But Göran had the advantage of not hearing his prodigious snoring, which kept me sleepless in addition to fishless, notwithstanding the three-timber rooms, occupied by what must have been mystified and miserable fishermen spending their own nights sleepless between us.

Sometime during our third week on the river, the rain let up, the wind lay down and the river considered returning to its banks. I had just fished 4 a.m. to 4 a.m. and had missed the daily phone call from the San Diego spa, so I headed back to the lodge, spooking mother oystercatchers that frantically feigned broken wings to lead me from their chicks. The hedgehog couple cuddled in the darkless summer night under the stairs to the lodge knew I was friendly and never acknowledged me.

Jammed in my door was a note from Göran saying: "The Blonde Flicka telephone, say she has leaved spa for sailing. Cannot telephone from sailboat. Will meat [sic] in airport as planned." I should have suspected that the Golden Door hosted singles' weeks for meat fishermen.

Göran called her the "Blonde Flicka" ever since I had persuaded him—by means of an invitation to fish a fair beat on the Gaula, a wader bag of Snickers bars, the promise of a couple of weeks on the Homosassa flats, and finally a good deal of nonspecific begging—to teach my bride to cast a two-handed rod on our honeymoon 12 months earlier. I knew how lucky I had been that he finally acceded to all my importuning. Fishing with him previously, I overheard him refuse repeated requests from Prince Charles's equerry to teach Diana to cast. (Probably would have done HRH no more good keeping his bride out of mischief than it did me with mine.)

While the weather improved, the fishing did not, at least for me, though Göran, who can coax salmon from raging fosse or damp lawn, belabored my lack of success through his. I missed talking with the Blonde Flicka but, to be honest, I spent most of the balance of my trip either fishing or too exhausted to try to find her.

* * *

IT'S A LONG TRIP FROM FINNMARK TO Matapédia, but I was charged by the prospect of a big Restigouche fish to break my run of blank days. After the morning session, I drove back to Presque Isle through which I had just traveled, to collect the Blonde Flicka. That flights into northern Maine's unpredictable weather are unreliable is well known and to this I attributed her delay. During the three hours I waited, her scheduled flight and several others landed and left; if I waited much longer, I'd miss the bewitching hour when the sun at the fabled home pool goes down behind the mountain and the big salmon come up for tiny waked flies. Deflated, I headed back to the river.

I went into the rod room to grab the 13-foot Loop prototype Göran had designed. Rolled up in the stripping guide was a note: "Mr. Goodman— Your wife left the following phone message: 'Sweetheart, I love you deeply, but not so desperately as I hate salmon fishing.'"

This left me confused, scared and sad. Really sad. And it gave me a bellyache. Three times I had to tie the turle knot on the size 12 Blue Charm before I had it right. The 12-pounder that took it didn't make me feel much better. Not until the last cast of the evening, when the 22-pound hen snatched my size 14 Green-Butt hitching in the moonlight did I think I just might survive.

## Note on the Author

David L. Goodman of Great Falls, Virginia is a mortgage banker in nearby Reston. David is a volunteer officer in the North Atlantic Salmon Fund. He lives alone with Comet, his white Westie terrier, and 382 fly rods.

# Coincidence— or Curse?

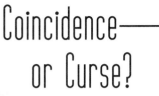

By Alysse E. Hollis

I AM A LAWYER. I AM, THEREFORE, PRONE TO thinking in terms of hypotheticals. Whenever I go on a fishing trip with Josh, I play an elaborate hypothetical game with myself that I like to call, "How Close To Dead Would I Have To Be Before My Husband Would Stop Fishing And Get Me Proper Medical Attention?" The answer—and the duration and intensity of my hypothetical suffering—depend on a variety of factors.

How far did we have to travel to get to our location? Do we plan to spend more than one day there? How many fish were caught prior to my hypothetical deadly injury? Are there other people in the vicinity who are not fishing and are thus available to transport me to the nearest medical facility? Can the deadly injury be at least temporarily addressed by one or more of the items in our first-aid kit? Is my injury self-inflicted, e.g., did it occur because I insisted on wading in my flip flops rather than my wading boots?

And the kicker: Is my hypothetical death so imminent that even if my husband stopped fishing immediately there would be no hope of saving my life?

I met Josh five years ago when I moved back to Denver after attending law school in California. He had moved to Denver from the Midwest to fly fish. We have since moved to northern Kentucky, where, shortly after our arrival, what should open practically down the street but a new fly shop? It's northern Kentucky's first and only fly shop.

Coincidence ... or curse?

Josh and I had been dating for a few months when several of his relatives decided to come out to Colorado and rent a cabin in Leadville for a week. This was to be the first time I would meet Josh's family, including his sister Erica and her then-boyfriend Robbie. I was nervous and excited. I liked this guy, and I wanted his family to like me. We had planned it so that each night, one couple was responsible for the dinner, which meant that each couple had to cook the meal and then clean up afterward. Josh and I were to make burritos (*his* specialty) on our second night in the cabin.

That morning, Josh and Robbie decided to explore a few local fishing spots Josh had spotted on our trip up to Leadville. Note that this was early in the morning. By nightfall they still had not returned. The burrito plans were scrapped; Erica and I ended up making spaghetti and getting drunk on cheap beer as we commiserated over our common fate. Josh and Robbie straggled in after dark, sheepish, but unapologetic, with the classic "we lost track of time" excuses.

It was clear to both Erica and me that to Josh and Robbie the day of fishing had been worth our wrath. No matter what we said or did, it wouldn't change anything. We couldn't win this—it was bigger than us.

\* \* \*

I WOULD BET THAT IF JOSH AND I TRIED TO think back over the years, we'd discover that pretty much every event of any significance in our relationship involves fishing. For instance, any kind of travel, whether it's a vacation, a weekend getaway or merely the act of getting from one place to another, will almost certainly be combined with fishing, or at the very least *attempted* fishing.

I'll look over at Josh any time we drive near a body of water and I'll notice his eyes drift away from the road. He's trying to figure out: A) what the possibility is that there are fish in that water, and B) the severity of the fit I'll throw if he stops to find out. It doesn't matter whether the water in question is a muddy pond in someone's yard or the Mississippi River—I can see him analyze the fishing potential. Then he'll start with the bargaining. He'd like to stop for a minute, just to see if there are any fish in there. Just a couple of casts—would I mind? As if I'm going to fall for this.

Just a couple of casts. *And then what?* What if there are fish in there? We're going to turn around and get back in the car, go on to our destination, happy in the knowledge that we found fish? Well, no, of course not. If there are fish in there, then we must try to catch them.

It must have been around the time of the Leadville trip—although I don't remember the exact moment—that I realized that I was in love with a man who would never love me as much as he loved fly fishing. I certainly realized from the beginning that he placed a high priority on the sport and ranked it, in order of importance, up there with breathing and eating, and well above sleeping.

If one were to apply Maslow's famous hierarchy of needs to Josh, fly fishing would have to be included as one of those physiological needs: the ones at the bottom. The ones without which the person will die. I have always suspected that Josh's self-proclaimed "hobby" might be closer to something of an obsession and maybe even an addiction. After all, the signs of addiction are all there: the impaired judgment *("Honey, you won't mind if I go on a three-day fishing trip instead of going with you to your firm's summer party that you told me about six months ago ... right?")*; the distorted sense of reality *("I'm going fishing for a couple hours"* means at least five hours, and more likely eight to 10); and, of course, the blackouts *("Really? I was gone that long? It didn't seem like that long")*.

I do have to admit that I somewhat envy the simplicity that being an avid angler brings to Josh's life. Josh never has to think twice when asked the question others often dread, "So what do you like to do in your spare time?" Now, I think I'm a pretty complex person and I like to do lots of different things in my spare time. How am I supposed to answer that? Josh on the other hand can simply say, "I fly fish."

Done.

\* \* \*

ONCE I CALLED JOSH FROM SAN FRANCISO where I was attending a friend's wedding. He had to stay behind in Colorado because he couldn't get the time off work to go to the wedding because all his vacation time had already been used up on our "honeymoon" (call it what you will—it was a fishing trip dressed up to look like a honeymoon). I asked what he was doing and he said he was going out for pizza. "Oh, that's cool," I said, "with whom?"

"With Andy," he said.

"Who the hell is Andy?"

"Oh, he's this guy I met fishing the Tomahawk today. He's really cool. I invited him and his girlfriend over for drinks next weekend. You'll really like her."

"Oh, you met his girlfriend too?"

"No, but he told me about her and she sounds like someone you'd like."

And this is how simple it is for Josh. If you meet someone fly fishing, he's a friend. And if his wife or girlfriend puts up with it, then she's *my* friend. I mean, we already know we'll have something in common, right?

I also must admit that if fly fishing is an addiction, I am probably something of a fishing "enabler." Every birthday, every Christmas, I'm there at the local fly shop buying books, waders, tools, rods, reels, classes, club memberships, you name it. If it has to do with fly fishing, I either have given it as a gift or will give it as a gift to my husband. What else can I give him that will make him happy? One Christmas a couple of years ago I gave him a nice leather jacket. It's never been worn. The Sage rod I gave him—now that's seen a lot of use. But aren't I really sealing my fate every time I give him a gift? Would I buy a fifth of whiskey for my husband if he was an alcoholic? Isn't this the same thing? Is Josh a "fishaholic?" Perhaps several of us fishing widows should start a support group. We could call it FISH: Forgetful, Inconsiderate, Selfish Husbands. Maybe we could find a recovered fishaholic to start some kind of treatment program. Fish-Anon? And then there's the real question: Can a true fishaholic ever recover?

On those rare occasions that I am frustrated enough or stupid enough to try to discuss Josh's addiction with him, his response is always that there are worse things he could do. I call this the "at-least-it's-not-drugs-or-hookers" rationale. While I am no doubt glad that at least it isn't drugs or hookers, I'm not sure he isn't missing the point. While his addiction hasn't (yet) left him bankrupt or in jail, I'm not certain that a lifelong fishing addiction, if left untreated, couldn't ruin a family, or at least a relationship, just as thoroughly as a drug addiction. This is why I decided early on in our relationship that I would have to learn to meet Josh half way.

I'm not suggesting this will work for everyone (and here I'm thinking particularly of those whose spouses may actually *be* addicted to drugs or hookers), but it seems to work for us. Although I had never fished a day in my life before I met Josh, I now enjoy fly fishing—to a point. I will never spend days at a time, from sunrise to sunset, in waders. But as I get better at the sport, I am starting to understand what could drive someone to do just that. In the meantime, it gives us a chance to spend time together. He's happy and, even if I'm not always having the time of my life, it is no longer the case that every fishing experience leaves me wet, cussing, mad and miserable. There are still times when I'd prefer finding the perfect pair of slingbacks on sale at the mall to catching a 20-inch trout. But at least I'm beginning to understand why, for my husband, the thrill is roughly the same.

\* \* \*

IN THE END, DESPITE THE COUNTLESS HOURS I have spent imagining a fitting end for my husband while I either burn to a crisp on a flats skiff somewhere in the tropics or freeze to death by the side of the road in a blizzard while he checks out some mountain stream, would I trade my life with a Josh for something different? I doubt it. After all, I don't have too many really great memories that involve dinners in fancy restaurants or black-tie social events. I do, however, have vivid (if not always fond) memories of almost every fishing trip Josh and I have ever taken, of all the special places we've discovered together and the people we've met through fishing.

What woman can say she got engaged while fishing in a snowstorm outside of Salida, Colorado, and that their husband had stashed the ring in his fly box, insisting, despite my protests to the contrary, that this "new fly" would make me forget all about my impending hypothermia? Who else can say she spent her honeymoon as the only guests at the Andros Island Bonefish Club because she and her new husband were the solitary couple crazy enough to go fishing in the Caribbean during hurricane season?

I will always remember the fun we had hiking through Colorado's Flat Top wilderness and fishing the streams that feed Trapper's Lake every Fourth of July weekend. I will always remember how our dog Grace, now gone, used to somehow know every time one of us caught a fish and would swim over to give it one nervous little lick before watching it swim away. I will always remember the white sand beaches of the Yucatán and the great people we met there. I will always be able to picture the stillness of Spinney Reservoir as the sun comes up. Of course, it's not always easy to remember these wonderful experiences when I'm waiting at home having spent hours cooking a dinner which is now getting cold because Josh lost track of time ... again. But I guess the fact that I stick around, knowing I can count on it happening time after time, means he must be worth it.

### Note on the Author

Alysse E. Hollis of Cincinnati, Ohio, is an attorney whose ideal fishing spot is adjacent to a white powder sand beach stretching beyond the horizon, and where frozen margaritas are delivered hourly with a smile.

# The Jealous Mistress

By Georgene S. Dreispoon

"PRIORITY" IS A POTENT WORD IN MOST relationships. Nothing challenges priority more than a sports compulsion; in our family it was fishing.

We joke about compulsions, but the term "fishing widow" says it all. The fisherman isn't dead—just caught up in his priority. I empathize with the fishing widow. I was there as a single woman and as a young wife. What changed my priority was parenthood. It was during the parenting period that my husband and I had our best fights; I was determined not to become a fishing widow, yet he was determined to fish. What follows is the essence of a fishing marriage rated PG.

I was a fisher-girl who became a fisher-woman, then a fisher-wife. For the sake of documentation, there's 53 years of mileage on the wife. At the age of 10, I was introduced to fishing by an angling Uncle Jack, a jovial, bespectacled dentist whose love for children shone behind his glasses. Uncle wanted someone to row him around the local ponds in quest of bass, perch and bluegill; I was just old enough to be trained for the task.

On our first outing he tutored me in the art of rowing. He said I should treat rowing as an intellectual challenge and gave me the impression the fish had the intelligence of Einstein and the sensitivity of a radar trap. Obediently, I rowed his boat and with calculated effort attempted to glide it slowly and quietly through the water. I was sure that the fish had ears turned toward the patterned ripples we discharged.

Uncle's strategy was to keep the girl quiet so he could indulge in the meditation prompted by a secluded pond on a clear summer day. I can still remember the evergreens surrounding us, and the distant island that broke the pond's surface.

Suddenly, a shriek shattered our silent pursuit. "Fish! I've got him! He's on!" Uncle shouted. "FISH, FISH, *FISH*" echoed around us. He scared the peace right out of me. Most of that day, I perched on the edge of my seat anxiously awaiting his next outburst. I sensed, at that young age, that fishing was a deceptive game.

He rewarded me later in the day by transferring his rod to me and patiently giving me casting instructions. He said the fish were just waiting to be caught; all I had to do is cast the plug to the right spot. I cast and cast and cast. Nothing happened. I learned then that arousing one's expectations is fundamental to this sport. He was priming me for my future role as a fisher-wife.

There are fishermen and there are fishermen. Uncle was a boatman who came equipped with plugs and live bait; how he fished depended on how the spirit moved him. He was a go-for-the-limit man. I loved him and thought this was a wonderful philosophy. I didn't find out until much later that there is a hierarchy in the fishing world and Uncle's lack of discrimination in his choice of method put him near the bottom.

\* \* \*

MY REVELATION CAME AT AGE 20 WHEN I MET a young fishing-doctor. He was an emerging fly fisher, probably at the nymph state, and determined to climb to the top. Fishermen know what that means. For those in doubt, I'll tell you in one sentence: He was possessed!

My first clue was when he casually mentioned that he had first examined our local trout streams, found them excellent, and then thought it made good sense to hatch a match with a local woman. He was raised as a city sportsman with the accompanying restrictions. Now he was looking for a country community that would welcome a young obstetrician and provide door-side fishing. When he explored the Hudson Valley, he found me. I was the farmer's daughter and the farmer conveniently owned a private, well-stocked lake.

With his first cast in my direction he expressed his desire to practice medicine where trout streams radiate from hospital centers. With the verbal casts that followed he exhibited an ability to lure. Then came a cast with a very fine leader: He asked me if I would like to inspect the neck of a jungle cock. His father had passed it down to him, he told me enthusiastically. Now it was on the endangered list. How could I resist? We went through his collection of special feathers. I was impressed. Also, the more I saw of him the more he reminded me of the actor Gene Kelly, minus the dancing feet.

I was hooked—pun intended.

Now it was my turn to use some seductive bait. "I *love* fishing!" was a good tempter; "Will you teach me to fly fish?" was even better; and "I can appreciate your need to get away from it all on a stream," was my treble hook.

Irving and I have always been sports enthusiasts with triple choices for each season. He had attended college on a basketball scholarship before discovering fishing and hunting. I hit every team my high school offered and added a few more in college. My picture in the high school yearbook sprouted a caption in bold letters—AMAZON—and I'm only five feet three inches tall. Until the late 1950s, femininity was considered incompatible with athletics. I figured most women just didn't know what they were missing.

But even an Amazon has difficulty dashing off to a stream whenever the spirit moves her, especially when she has three children within four years, all clamoring for attention. Irving and I often locked horns over his determination to spend his limited free time on the water. For many years fishing controlled him like a jealous mistress. I felt I could have competed with another woman, but how do you compete with a fish?

I tried. I trained the kids to suck in their cheeks and pucker their lips; we would line up together like guppies and bargain for his time. I strained for family participation, but the logistics with children made it difficult. We couldn't always go fishing when Dad wanted to go. Winter wasn't even a reprieve. There was ice fishing.

We had our share of go-arounds over fishing, while fishing and when planning fishing. When the dust settled, I discovered these confrontations had provided fertile compost for humor. One day there was a fishing incident that affected his professional life and brought us both insight and a spirit of compromise.

\* \* \*

IT WAS APRIL FIRST, THE OPENING OF TROUT season in New York State. The day was bitterly cold and damp. The sky threatened snow. My husband and a fishing buddy, the local district attorney, decided they had to grab a few hours of fishing even though they were both on call. My husband asked me to monitor the phone with instructions to call a colleague in the event of an emergency. The district attorney's wife—also struggling with the "fishing widow" syndrome—was in the same boat.

They were gone just one hour when the answering service called. A patient was in labor with her fifth child. For the medically uninformed, this means her baby was about to be released into the world like a struggling emerger becoming a dun. I was contemplating my next move when my phone rang again. It was the district attorney's wife. There had been a murder in a local bar and they needed her husband before they could remove the corpse from the barroom floor. She and I commiserated. We agreed we should call the state troopers to locate our husbands who were somewhere along the Beaverkill River. They were found with ice in their guides. The corpse waited. The baby didn't.

* * *

EVERYONE NEEDS TO GET AWAY SOMETIME, especially people with intense work pressures. A solo obstetrical practice is probably as intense a job as you can find. We compromised: 51 percent for him, 49 percent for me. I felt he was entitled to the extra percentage point, which was designated as a week to go fishing on his own with buddies. I had no idea when we made this plan how constructive this week would be to our relationship. I was still under 30, he had a five-year advantage, and we both had much learning ahead.

My husband and his friends planned their first May trip. Their excitement was contagious. Those of us classified as homebodies salivated at visions of landlocked salmon and brook trout filling our freezers. We women agreed that this culinary promise provided some justification for

their indulgence. The destination was Moose-
head Lake, Maine. They left the Hudson Valley
at 5 a.m. like a group of bandits, leaving four
wives, 10 kids, and the confusion of everyday
life. My log went like this:

Day One—I am very angry and jealous.

Day Two—I am adapting to his absence
and thinking generously that his getting away
is a good idea.

Day Three—I am planning my newfound
free time. I hadn't realized how much I organized my day around him.

Day Four—I am ecstatic: My freedom
seems luxurious. I'm glad he took off!

Day Five—I am beginning to feel that my
bed is a lonely place.

Day Six—I miss him; my bed is a lonely
place.

Day Seven—Fish dinners be damned, I
can't wait until he walks through that door.

When the men arrived, each had a week's
growth of beard, their limits of fish, and evidence
on their faces of happy camaraderie. The impact of
that week was a turning point for me.

\* \* \*

MARRIAGE DOES SET CERTAIN RESTRICTIONS on an individual's freedom. It's the compromises that make it work. However, marriage and sports have much in common. They both offer a spiritual and physical mystery that is exciting to explore but can never be completely resolved because of the ever-changing components—some as delicate as the bubbles on a stream. Age, health, finances, employment, family responsibilities, drive—they are enough to challenge any Amazon. If the physical chemistry sparks and both are committed, we grow with our mates and make the necessary adjustments.

We are now labeled statistical fossils. When you are married 53 years, that's what happens. It wasn't easy to become a fossil. It took one hell of a lot of hard work. There are many ingredients that go into making a successful fishing marriage. My husband is quick to point out that the adhesive ingredient in ours has been my sense of humor.

What does humor have to do with fishing or with sports in general?

Everything, if your sports partner happens to be your husband or wife. As for taking care of yourself, fishermen love the proverb from an Assyrian tablet dated 2000 B.C.: "The gods do not subtract from the allotted span of men's lives the hours spent in fishing." If you fish enough, you can live to be 100. If you do it right, you'll be smiling all the way.

Through the years, I've shared fishing stories with other wives. Statistically, we represent about one-third of the line-floggers. The majority of us do not fish for the same reasons men do, even though our men wish we did. Of course, there are exceptions, but most of us who have shouldered tents and forded streams have done so for the love of our mates—and what's wrong with that?

In some sports it is important for intensity of interest and skills to match; the beauty of fishing is its flexibility. The true sport, male or female, uses 30-pound-test line to bring in a fish weighing 100 pounds, and scores with patience and understanding.

## Note on the Author

Georgene S. Dreishspoon of Boynton Beach, Florida, lives with her husband, retired physician Irving Dreishpoon. She is the author of the book, *How to Hook Your Spouse*, available upon special order at Waldenbooks.

# Dolores in Belize

By James. H. Hall

YOU CAN'T BUY LOVE—EVEN I KNOW THAT. BUT I wasn't trying to buy love. I just wanted to purchase the naming rights to our trip to Belize. "This will be a 'fishing trip,'" I explained to my beloved—let's call her Dolores. That was fine with her, or so she said at the time.

I had some leverage: Dolores was recently divorced and could not afford a trip to Belize, and I could, or so I thought. This dates the trip to early 2000, the eve of the stock-market crash. The "wealth effect," plus my feelings for Dolores, a young statuesque brunette with captivating blue eyes, had left me in a state of "irrational exuberance." The market was a source of endless revenues, Dolores was my woman, and the world was my oyster. I should have known better.

\* \* \*

THE FIRST SIGN OF TROUBLE AROSE ON THE Miami-to-Belize City leg of the flight. While I slept, Dolores became infatuated with a man in the next aisle. Apparently they had made eye contact. When I woke up, she pointed him out to me.

"Yeah?" I mumbled, barely awake.

"He is *so* good looking," she gushed.

"Oh, okay." On second glance, I supposed he did have a sort of Ricardo Montalbon look about him. It so happened that the man was also bound for Ambergris Cay, and his mere presence on the same small island gave rise to a running fantasy: Would she by chance see him in San Pedro? Each trip to town was preceded by elaborate, fanciful speculation: suppose she saw him—suppose he said hello? Suppose he offered her a drink? Dolores has a good imagination and a sense of humor, and the way she carried on was amusing; it made me laugh. The trouble was that I was not supposed to be amused. I was supposed to be jealous. Maybe (I argued later in my defense) if we had been at home, I would have been jealous.

*"Maybe?"*

"No, I *would* have been. I would have been furious. I would have pounded him. I would've done something! You're damn right I would have!"

"Nice try, Jim."

\* \* \*

WE STAYED AT EL PESCADOR, A FISHING LODGE on the north end of Ambergris Cay, which is separated from the more developed south end and the town of San Pedro by a channel between islands. The lodge is nestled in a grove of coconut palms, between which brightly colored hammocks were suspended like ornaments. There is a swimming pool, with a teak deck, beach chairs and bar service. A white sand beach, raked clean each morning, leads to a long pier that reaches out into the blue lagoon. There is a palm-thatched gazebo at the end of the pier, where you can sit and gaze out at the surf pounding the coral reef, and beyond the reef at the dark blue waters of the Atlantic. If you cannot enjoy yourself at El Pescador, see your doctor.

Bright and early the next morning, I went fishing. Dolores went shopping in San Pedro. I was back by 3 p.m., at which point Dolores received my full, undivided attention—and not just mine. "Hey, you changed your outfit," one guy said to her, as we entered the bar. "But you still look great!"

We sat off to one side. "What's that all about?" I asked.

"I have no idea. I think he's had a few."

Then we had a few, then dinner at a large table with our newly minted friends. The food was abundant, the seafood fresh. Bonhomie and fishing stories flowed freely. The beauty of a fishing lodge is that you *always* have something in common with your companions, and that something is *always* fishing. You don't have to waste time searching for common conversational ground

Dolores had a wonderful time. I know because I asked her frequently, "Are you having a good time?"

And always the same enthusiastic answer, "You *know* I am."

I did know. She bought gifts in San Pedro; she snorkeled the second largest barrier reef in the world; she made excursions by boat, plane and bus to the Belize City zoo, to Mayan ruins, to Guatemala. And one day she came bonefishing with me. "The best day of all," she called it. I agreed.

Dolores worshipped the sun. She loved the flats, the mangroves, the birds—we saw a roseate spoonbill—the beautiful water, the many shades of blue and green. For a while she stood on the bow with me watching the marine life, the graceful rays, small lethargic lemon sharks and not so small barracuda. I wanted her to see a bonefish before and after it was hooked, to see what all the fuss was about, but bonefish were hard to find and even harder to hook. There were more boats than I remembered from previous trips, and the fish were more skittish than ever.

Mid-morning on *our* day on the water, we staked out on Con Grejo, Crab Key. Dolores was sitting down now, reading her book or just soaking up the sun. She looked happy; every time I caught her eye she smiled. I know I was happy: It was late winter, and I was standing in the warm sun on the bow of a flats boat staked out on my favorite key, with an agreeable guide, June, beside me, and Dolores sunning contentedly a few feet away. Lunch was in the cooler, all was right with the world. Then it got even righter.

"There!" said June, "at 11 o'clock. Some bonefish are coming."

"I see them." The fish were suspended in the middle depth of water that wasn't quite as shallow as we had been fishing, so the fish weren't quite as spooky. They were coming directly toward us. A flip cast of maybe 20 feet was all that was required. Immediately the lead fish surged forward. I gave the line a little tug with my fingers, felt the resistance, and released and cleared the slack line as the fish bolted and the reel made a very satisfying, high-pitched whine. Dolores came forward to watch. "Wow," she said.

"It's really something, isn't it?"

"Amazing."

The guide sat on the gunwale as I worked the fish. Dolores stood beside me just the way I had envisioned it. I hoped that if she saw what I saw, she would feel what I felt, or at least have a better appreciation of why I felt as I did about bonefishing. I was looking for what I believe they call the "objective correlative." What I found was a pathetic fallacy. I should have learned from my sons that, even when you show a non-angler a fish, you cannot expect the same flood of adrenaline or endorphins—or whatever it is that defines a fisherman—from them. It is not learned behavior. It is biologic. Learned behavior would be recognizing that you cannot get non-angler excited about fish, *any* fish. I was a slow learner.

The guide found the perfect place for lunch: a sun-drenched lagoon with a hard sand bottom, with a palette of blues and greens stretching to the horizon. Dolores and I ate sandwiches and drank our tea, and then we slithered over the side like a pair of seals and swam around cooling off and relieving ourselves. Then we clambered back aboard. I fished until the early afternoon, but when the light changed and the wind lifted, the magic left too. It was time to reel in. Soon, the week was over and it was time to go home.

\* \* \*

DID I MENTION THAT DELORES AND I WORKED in the same office? That's how we met but, for the most part, Dolores and I had separate circles of friends at work. My friends were mostly men, and what we usually talked about were sports, specifically the Red Sox, Patriots and Celtics. Dolores's closest friends were women, and usually they discussed relationships.

The relationships my friends and I most often discussed were the ones between Carl Everett, a contentious Red Sox centerfielder, and his coach, or Patriot quarterback Drew Bledsoe's relationship with the media. Among my friends, Red Sox gossip took precedence over my trip with Dolores. Not so with Dolores's friends. Her friends had been quite interested in the trip, particularly in whether I took "even a single day" off from fishing to spend with her.

"I wasn't going to lie to them," Dolores said.

This was the first time it had been mentioned. "Did you *want* me to take time off?" I asked.

"It might have been nice."

"But you never asked! You never even hinted."

She shrugged as if to say, she shouldn't have had to ask.

"I'm not a mind reader." An old argument that I always lost. "This isn't fair," I said. "You're revising history. At the time you said you were having fun. Every time I asked."

"I *was* having fun. I had a great time. You know that."

"It doesn't sound like it."

"If you're going to get all defensive, I'll quit sharing things with you."

"Maybe you should."

This wasn't about money. Okay, it was *a little* about money, because six days of guided fishing was part of the package. Not to fish was to toss money away. More importantly, not to fish would have squandered an entire precious day on the flats. To a fly fisher, unless he lives in the tropics or is ridiculously wealthy, each day on the flats is priceless, irreplaceable. If he is *lucky,* a man is allocated a few such days in a lifetime. To squander even one seems sinful.

But once a relationship goes south, figuratively speaking—once the woman comes to believe that she has been mistreated—that's the ball game. Time to haul out all the other charges, including, unbelievably, that on the return trip I had been observed ogling a tall Asian woman's legs in the Belize

City airport—which, aside from the meretricious use of "ogling"—may have been true, but was beside the point.

"So what if I did 'glance' at her legs? Compared to your behavior on the flight down with that sleazy..."

"It's not the same. Because it doesn't bother you. You thought it was funny."

\* \* \*

IT WAS NO USE. NOW MY SENSE OF HUMOR was being used against me: ogling, non-jealousy, too much fishing, etc. etc. As Dolores summarized in her closing arguments, "You blew it, Jim."

And I guess I did, because I always naively believed that a passion for fly fishing was a personal attribute, a positive character trait. Now to have it held against me, especially retroactively, seemed grossly unfair. It still does. Imagine Drew Bledsoe relaxing in the locker room, after what he thought was a good game, a victory, only to have the referees come in a while later and inform him that "upon further review" of the video, several calls on the field had been reversed. Turns out that he had a false start and stepped out of bounds; none of the touchdowns counted. He had played a lousy game and he had lost. At least in the NFL, you can appeal to the league office. I had no recourse whatsoever, and it wasn't too long after the Belize trip that Dolores gave me my release.

Later I licked my wounds and tallied up my losses. By my calculations, Dolores's share of the trip came to about $2,500. If instead of taking her to Belize, I had invested that in blue chip stocks, such as Lucent, Nortel or Enron— okay, financially it was a wash. And, money aside, I came out ahead, because the truth is that I had a *wonderful* time with Dolores in Belize, a much better time than I would have had without her. And I believe her when she says that she had a good time too, a *great* time. It was only *we* who didn't fare so well, because, in fact, there wasn't any we. She and I just hadn't realized yet.

### Note on the Author

James H. Hall of Jay, Maine, says that when he took up fly fishing more than 30 years ago, he thought he had found something more difficult to comprehend than women: "Boy, was I wrong—by a mile." He is the author of *Cover Girl & Other Stories of Fly-Fishermen in Maine.*

# Fly Fishing
# with the Girl Next Door

## By Thomas R. Pero

MY QUIXOTIC VISION EVAPORATED WHEN she joined our fly-fishing club. I was planning to spend my life in monastic devotion to bamboo rods, mayfly identification, and perfecting the classic divided wood-duck wing dry fly. I was 18. She was 37.

Call her Mrs. Robinson. She was lean with blue eyes and short blond hair. She was anxious and smoked Kool cigarettes. She dressed in tight, worn Levis and chambray work shirts with the sleeves rolled up. She didn't wear makeup. She liked strong coffee made from boiling water poured through freshly ground beans into a Chemex carafe (I had seen neither the ritual nor tasted true coffee before).

She was originally from San Francisco, she told me. She smiled when she talked about dancing on her high-school gymnasium floor in stocking feet with the future singer, Johnny Mathis. She adored Joan Baez and listened to John Denver. She asked if I had read Annie Dillard's *Pilgrim at Tinker Creek*. (No, but I could quote from Harold Blaisdell's *The Philosophical Fisherman*.) She had married young but had gotten out quickly. The second time around she had married her Jewish psychiatrist, with whom she now lived comfortably in a fashionable suburb of Boston. They had twin 10-year-old daughters, both spoiled rotten. The children routinely threw tamper tantrums by falling to the polished hardwood floor, legs kicking and fists pounding, and wailing, "I think I'm going crazy!" Discipline might have given them a complex.

She longed to be a liberated woman of the 1970s yet detested him for needing his money. She probably would have made a perfectly content Montana ranch wife, living in an Ivan Doig novel. The *faux* gaslights and pretentious boutiques along Newberry Street made her claustrophobic. She was happier in hip boots up to her knees in the muddy ooze of an inky beaver pond, casting for six-inch brook trout. Among legions of the desperate housewives of her generation, she swallowed the then-all-the-rage Erica Jong's *Fear of Flying* as scripture:

And what about those other longings which marriage stifled? Those longings to hit the open road from time to time, to discover whether you could still live alone inside your own head, to discover whether you could manage to survive in a cabin in the woods without going mad; to discover, in short, whether you were still whole after so many years of being half of something (like the back two legs of a horse outfit on the vaudeville stage). Five years of marriage had made me itchy for all those things: itchy for men, and itchy for solitude. Itchy for sex and itchy for the life of a recluse. I knew my itches were contradictory—and that made things worse. I knew my itches were un-American—and that made things *still* worse. It is heresy in America to embrace any way of life except as half a couple. Solitude is un-American....

Even more to the point: the woman (unhappy though she knows her married friends to be) can never let *herself* alone. She lives as if she were constantly on the brink of some great fulfillment. As if she were waiting for Prince Charming to take her away "from all this." All what? The solitude of living inside her own soul? The certainty of being herself instead of half of something else?

My response to all this was not (not yet) to have an affair and not (not yet) to hit the open road, but to evolve my fantasy of the Zipless Fuck. The zipless fuck was more than a fuck. It was a platonic ideal. Zipless because when you came together zippers fell away like rose petals, underwear blew off in one breath like dandelion fluff. Tongues intertwined and turned liquid. Your whole soul flowed out through your tongue and into the mouth of your lover.

For the true, ultimate zipless A-1 fuck, it was necessary that you never get to know the man very well....

Well, then. Somewhere in the process of sorting all this out she decided to take up fly fishing.

"What about your husband?" I asked in a spontaneous lava flow of passion—tongues intertwined and turning liquid, as Ms. Jong had salaciously conjured—while spring peepers serenaded us from the skunk-cabbage swamp outside the car window near the old rod-and-gun club.

"He's screwing his secretary," said Mrs. Robinson matter of factly.

"Oh," I said.

She had negotiated two days a week off from household routine: Tuesday and Thursday. At the time I was putting 58-cents-a-gallon gas in my car to make runs down the Cape for salters and buying the occasional Fenwick Feralite fiberglass rod (I knew where to get a deal, at Dick's in Dighton) by tying flies commercially, a baker's dozen at a time. That summer I didn't get many orders filled Tuesdays and Thursdays. She had only one rule: Not in her house.

She typically showed up mid-morning, once my mother was safely installed at her desk in the medical records office of the local hospital downtown. We headed off to fish one or another local stream, flowing through rough oaks and smooth beeches and bordered with radiant islands of yellow marsh marigolds. Sometimes we ended up panting on a carpet of white-pine needles. There was always the car. Or my mother's new living room sofa. Or the downstairs leatherette sofa in the family recreation room. Sometimes my twin bed, where not too many years earlier I had stared at the delusory pages of a contraband copy of *Playboy* with my Boy Scout mini-light under the sheets or lain awake past midnight listening with earphones (which I thought my mother didn't know I had but of course she did) when the perennially losing Red Sox were on the West Coast and the game started after my established bedtime. I wanted to be fireball reliever Dick Radatz.

Always amusing to both me and Mrs. R. was the ancient Portuguese man in the adjoining yard. Fragrant wisps of smoke from his pipe drifted through my screened bedroom window. He sat in his lawn chair, alternately dozing off and waking himself up with a grumbling snort, while mere feet away we were making a fury of the sheets. Alas, he posed no eavesdropping threat: He was as deaf as his white-washed fence posts.

We took her cherry-red family station wagon on a fly-fishing road trip. She told me to drive. I remember cruising along Interstate 89 through the lush Green Mountains in Vermont, while the church steeples of the White River valley whizzed by. I managed to stay in my lane, but was having a hard time concentrating. To the cars passing because of our vehicle's erratic progress—slowing down then speeding up—the irate drivers likely assumed the skinny solo youth at the wheel had popped one too many colored pills. This conclusion was probably confirmed as they looked over at my dreamy straight-ahead gaze, long hair, and gold-rimmed glasses. The driver in the cab of the much-higher 18-wheeler who down-shifted and gave me the thumbs-up sign got quite a different view. *Coo-coo-ca-choo.*

Compared with the infinitely complex—not to mention torturously unproductive—relationship games played by the Catholic high-school girls, this was more like it. So much for the vapid 17-year-olds! The contrast was sensational. I was a *big* fan of older women. I was bursting. I could have jumped through my own skin. I hadn't felt this secret thrill since I discovered I could drag the kitchen chair over and reach the Fudgsicles in the freezer all by myself.

She told me John Lennon used to drink some rot-gut called May wine, so I brought along several bottles and got ill drinking them. We fished a clear stream churning and cascading over the most amazing multicolored marble bedrock for the most exquisite wild rainbow trout. The tiny fish, miniature peels of quicksilver, came up as swiftly as any I had experienced to snatch my size 16 Adams dry fly as it sail-boated along. It was one of her favorite places in the world, she told me. She came here to sit and listen to the water music. She read me some forgettable poetry. Yeats and that Browning couple no longer seemed so petrified.

When the maple leaves started turning crimson and gold she gave me notice that it was over. "You have to move on," she told me, as gently as she could. I gave her a pastel drawing I had made of spawning brook trout and cried.

"You have your whole life ahead of you," she said. "I've made my choices and I have to live with them. There will be many interesting women in your life. They'll love you. Trust me."

Years later I heard she had moved out of the suburbs to the countryside, where she became romantically involved with the local game warden. She booted him out when she discovered he was simultaneously carrying on an affair with another woman across town. That was another one of her rules: one at a time. Mrs. Robinson taught me much. She was right, of course. Life's long float trip has indeed led me to many interesting women—some prettier, a few quirkier, precious few as honest, though none more gracious.

The Irish playwright George Bernard Shaw pretty much hit it on the money when he noted that youth is wasted on the young. I can honestly say, however, that the experience was an epiphany. I knew it at the time. It was my first thoroughly existential fly-fishing relationship. And I survived.

Here's to you, Mrs. Robinson.

* * *

"WAS ED EVER IN ANY KIND OF SERIOUS relationship—with a woman, I mean?" I asked a mutual friend of ours. Ed is a thoughtful, intelligent man in his 40s, with a fleeting resemblance to the actor Johnny Depp. Ed is notoriously single.

This may have some connection with his demanding personal schedule of 250 days a year up to his waist in chilled water, which if anything is an underestimate. Often the water is flowing through remote real estate in Alaska or Russia. When not on some far-flung adventure he's patrolling one of several local rivers in Washington, rain or shine, from dawn to dusk, or sleeping on frozen ground in a pup tent in 10-degree weather on the banks of a December river in British Columbia.

"Yeah," answered the friend. "He was married once, for about six months. But he never talks about it. I think it ended badly. She couldn't take it any more." On her way out the door the young lady, having finally shucked all illusion of the potential for a reality makeover, somberly informed Ed that he was sick, truly *sick*, addicted to fishing the way some people are addicted to cocaine. Or worse. She advised him to seek professional help.

Rid of whatever civilizing intrusion may have been distracting him, Ed promptly moved into a fishing companion's garage. Then he ordered up a sleek, custom-built aluminum jet sled costing half as much as a new Humvee, and happily parked the gleaming steelhead chariot outside his functional new abode, ready to go at a moment's notice.

Which reminds me of the time I was sitting in the audience of one of those fisheries-management symposia held every few years in Yellowstone, where all stripes of experts get together to impress each other with elaborate graphs and charts showing catch-rates and barbless-hook theories, while—several hundred miles away in Boise and Helena and Laramie—lobbyists with legislators obediently tethered are industriously contriving ever-more-creative ways of outlawing a trout stream's natural inclination to flow downhill. A speaker broke the monotony by announcing that human beings who tie artificial flies, then attach them to their fishing lines, then cast them with the intent of hooking a trout are certifiably obsessed. The man was a psychologist. He had recently conducted an organized series of interviews (this was long before the dubious "focus group" had entered the popular lingo) with gatherings of sportsmen: duck hunters, deer hunters, muskie fishers, smallmouth bass fishers, you name it. Yep, fly fishers are NUTS. They will let nothing stand in the way of their passionate pursuit: not career advancement, not more toys, not children, not domestic tranquility, not sexual escapades, not their homes, nor even their livelihoods. *Nothing.* Only bow hunters suffer—or apparently enjoy—a higher rate of divorce.

Evidence gathered during recent fieldwork suggests this universal bonfire of fly-fishing devotion rages merrily on. Last winter, while wading the flats on a tiny island in the middle of the Indian Ocean, I ran into a prosperous real-estate developer from the Ozarks who, despite having been late for his own wedding ceremony because he had innocently stopped to make a few casts, was miraculously still in a certified state of legal matrimony. Months earlier I observed an American fishing guide in Kamchatka, who had spent the entire summer and into autumn looking after anglers on wilderness rivers, invest a goodly portion of his meager take-home pay placing two satellite phone calls. The first was to see how the Red Sox were faring against the Yankees; the follow-up was to his seasonally abandoned wife—a registered nurse with a real job—to share with her the exciting news: Now that all the paying anglers had cleared out of camp, the steelhead were really pouring in. It was a great opportunity. He wouldn't be back in Missoula until sometime in November. After a long period of icy silence (at $15 a minute) she hung up on him. "She'll get over it," he said—somewhat optimistically, I thought. "I'll have all winter to hang around the house and run errands for her." This young man had his priorities.

Not all women object to fishing. Some genuinely love it. Others fish to catch or keep men. "A girl's gotta do what a girl's gotta do," a woman I once dated let slip after her second Chardonnay. Yet it is also my experience that women who take enthusiastically to the fly rod often become more adept at it than the men who introduced them to the sport.

The poseurs are easy to spot. One recalls images of Diana Spencer, the future Princess of Wales, fully "kitted out," as the Brits say, in shiny new Wellies and quilted vest, tentatively wielding an immense two-handed Hardy rod for the benefit of an army of cameramen, and exhibiting all the cheeriness of a corpse. No doubt she would have been far happier romping with the celebrity set on the sprawling lawns of Elton John's ostentatious Berkshire mansion, far from the pines of Balmoral and the slippery stones of the River Dee. But then one cannot imagine Sir Elton sashaying about in waders, unless, of course, Simms could be persuaded to produce a custom XXXL model hemmed with purple rhinestones. Diana went through the motions of fly fishing because her betrothed was devoted to it, not because she had any particular interest in perfecting her greased-line technique. As she later tattled to the lurid national tabloids, she found the Prince of Wales's fondness for the country life—for grouse shooting and walking on moors and such—pointless. Word is she later forbade Charles his traditional fortnight of salmon fishing on the Hofsá in Iceland. That tells you something right there. At best she was tempting the fates; at worst she was inviting bad karma. You don't keep a devout angler off his or her home water without consequence. You mess with Etain, the ancient Celtic goddess of water, at your own peril. Diana's mother-in-law's very own poet laureate, Ted Hughes—himself a true believer in the mystical powers of flowing water and fly fishing—could have told her that. The Princess of Wales lusted for international excitement. She got it.

In the same household, the Queen Mother, Prince Charles's beloved grandmum, was honestly smitten with fishing all her life, and was by all reliable accounts never more in her element than Deeside in springtime. She fished avidly until well into her 90s. An old gillie I met in Scotland told me how the Queen Mother favored a gin-and-tonic in the fishing hut as the customary start to a day's outing. Once she savored her drink to satisfaction, she walked from the hut a short distance to the water and commenced casting her favorite fly. In a while, if nothing was doing, she would come back and enjoy another drink, then resume fishing, and so on. When a salmon finally took, Her Highness raised her rod, presumably in salute, bracing for the great splashes and electrifying leaps that fresh-run Atlantic salmon typically display. The gillie would rush down to the river, grab the diminutive woman around the waist, hoist her out of the shallows and walk backward toward the retreat of the hut, the royal angler squealing with delight as the thrashing, yard-long silver fish was towed along for the rollicking ride to the riverbank.

There are few females willing to risk everything for fly fishing. Joan Salvato Wulff is uniquely at the head of the pack. A celebrated casting champion as a teenager during the Depression and an independent young entrepreneur during World War II, she grew up in a northern New Jersey family of sportsmen with the emphasis on men. She dreamed of a life of woodsmoke and running rivers. She ended up a suburban housewife. Then in the summer of 1966 Joan received a phone call from a fishing tackle company desperate for a petite (Joan was a slim five-foot-five) angler to fill in for popular singer Kay Starr, who had sung with Glenn Miller and Count Basie, and who now had taken ill in Las Vegas. Joan found herself in a small boat in the North Atlantic off Newfoundland trolling for giant bluefin tuna while cameras for ABC's *The American Sportsman* rolled. Cheerleading and helping rig her bait was well-known angler Lee Wulff, a swash-buckling outdoorsman who starred in his own films. More than two decades separated them. There was instant chemistry. Joan went home, filed for divorce, and married Wulff a year later. She packed up and moved her two teenage boys to a New Hampshire farmhouse. For Joan it was her second marriage, for Lee his fifth. Now Joan had a husband who knew a thing or two about fly rods himself, but also had the keys to a SuperCub airplane plus secret directions to a hidden place in Labrador where eight-pound brook trout slurped dry flies eagerly. The woman had her priorities.

Still, there are prominent fly fishers who remain unenthused about women in waders. On a radiant spring day, I once took a break for midday tea and whisky with the flamboyant English spey caster, Hugh Falkus, in his stone casting hut in Cumbria overlooking the Irish Sea. He had recently written a tongue-in-cheek introduction to a book postulating that the reason women held all the records for exceptionally large Atlantic salmon is because of a mysterious something called pheromones, which women and men exude distinctly.

"Mr. Falkus," I asked the ruddy-faced former RAF fighter pilot. "What do you think about the trend of more women getting into fly fishing?"

"I had a girlfriend," he pronounced the words as if ridding himself of ponderous weights, one by one, his silver mane of hair bristling above piercing blue eyes and hawk-like nose.

I taught her to spey cast. And she was a pretty as a picture. Jesus, God, she was a pretty girl. She was tall, slim and stood in a pair of breast waders like a fucking sea nymph, casting across the River Tweed. [At first] she was not a beautiful caster. I taught her. Jesus—how did I ever manage it? I don't know. In the end she became a wonderful caster, really wonderful. She would stand there absolutely still and—*whew!*—the line would shoot across the river. People would come and stand on the bridge just to watch her. But, you see, when we would get invited to fish all over the place, nearly always it was such expensive fishing that we would share a rod. And, oh dear, oh dear ... once

I'd taught her to cast properly, I didn't see much of the rod! Let her cater and cook the lunch and take care of the fish bag, but never let her get her hands on the rod.

"Why?" I goaded him.

"You'll never get it back!" he said with a laugh as he poured himself another tumbler of amber liquid. "Never, *never* marry a woman who fishes ... a woman will always steal the best pool. If you're sharing a rod, she'll have it for the rest of the day. You'll finish up gillying. I bloody know. I have a lifetime's experience."

Of course, the old man might not have been the most reliable source of balanced advice about relationships and women. Falkus claimed to have lived a happy heterosexual life ("I always said my wants were very simple: I want a pretty girl, a country cottage in the most idyllic surroundings that I could possibly find, a stretch of private salmon and sea trout fishing, and some shooting. I've got that. I can be happy. I've made sure that I have that."). But when I asked him how work was progressing on his next book about spey casting (his early book *Sea Trout* is an angling classic) he said: "I don't know what it's like in America, but it's pretty grisly over here. Nowadays, my dear Mr. Pero, I'll tell you, the whole scene has shifted in the publishing world. This is why this is going to be my last book. 'Cause the bloody women have moved in and taken over. All the magazines—nearly all of them—are taken up by women now. They've taken over the publishing houses. And, I'll tell you, what a set of bitches they are! Jesus Christ. Unless you're very good at getting on with a lot of lesbian bitches, I say to you, avoid the English publishing scene for as long as you can. It's no place to be."

He would not talk about his first marriage. Buried in a scrapbook of Falkus's scathing but frequently humorous pronouncements on this or that and letters from loyal fans, I spied a yellowed news clipping from *The Sentinel* about one Lady Marchioness of Londonderry. In pencil was written "late and unlamented."

In the photograph Lady Edith is draped in dazzling jewels, her head aglitter with a tiara so packed with diamonds it was known as the Family Fender. Before she fell out of popular favor for playing footsie with some world-class Bad Guys for the Ages, she was Britain's ultimate party gal. Her chief accomplishment was political hostess: Once a year on the eve of parliament she stood at the top of a magnificent staircase at Londonderry House in Park Lane, the Prime Minister of the day at her side, and received 2,000 fawning guests. She called Churchill "Winston the Warlock" and nick-named herself "Circe the Sorceress."

Before Munich, Lady Edith and her husband—described variously as an "upper-class twit" and "clueless, condescending, impossibly rich, impossibly refulgent in their own world"—accepted an invitation to visit Germany as the guests of Hermann Göring and Joachim von Ribbentrop. They were introduced personally to Hitler. Lady Edith was impressed, calling him a "man of arresting personality—a man with wonderful far-seeing eyes." She felt, she said, "in the presence of one truly great." Back on the British Isles, they placed a gift white porcelain statuette of a Nazi stormtrooper in the 78-acre garden surrounding their castles in Northern Ireland.

Summer of 1940: Twenty-one-year-old Hugh Falkus, after shooting down three London-bound German bombers in what came to be known as the Battle of Britain, watched a Messerschmidt turn his Spitfire to flaming, billowing rubble. Bleeding and in shock, he crash-landed in a French wood. Miraculously, he was alive. The young man was captured by SS thugs who danced up and down in front of him, shouting: "Pig! Swine! English shit!" Escorted at rifle point to an occupied farmhouse, a Luftwaffe officer offered him a surreal glass of champagne, apologizing for the coarseness of the stemware. During the next four years he survived ill-fed and often cold in a succession of grim prison camps in Germany, Poland, and Silesia. He worked on 13 tunnels, including one 340 feet long, and played a reluctant role in the spectacular failure later recreated by Hollywood as *The Great Escape*. He finally got out by cutting through the wire. He made his was back to England two weeks before Hitler committed suicide in 1945.

In the old newspaper clipping, under the picture captioned "Lord and Lady Londonderry in court dress, May 1935," Falkus had scrawled: "My Mother-in-Law! Jesus."

\* \* \*

SOME YEARS AGO AN OREGON FRIEND AND I invited a fellow from the East Coast to accompany us on a week-long fishing adventure in the Canadian wilds, hoping the experience would give him some quiet time to contemplate his rapidly unraveling marriage, in addition to providing some water-churning, lively sport for us. As we were waving good-bye to the helicopter, our visitor was already popping the cork on a bottle of Glenmorangie. As Eric and I rushed about setting up camp, our friend sat on a folding chair watching the steelhead river go by and proceeded to drain the bottle of two-thirds of its amber-colored contents. (It was one of those full-liter bottles from the duty-free border crossing.) Within an hour he was a blathering madman, alternately laughing at and belittling us for our lack of fishing prowess, while wallowing in tongue-addled, head-hung self-pity about his tenuous sleeping arrangements back in Rhode Island.

"Fishing is *the enemy!*" he howled like a banshee into the fading sunshine, summarizing his soon-to-be-ex-wife's regrettable attitude toward his life-long passion. Left out of the raving litany of lament was his long-running habit of keeping in close personal contact with serial mistresses, albeit, to the best of my knowledge, exclusively one at a time. The latest had in fact placed a perfume-sprinkled pair of panties in his fleece jacket for him to remember her by. This thoughtful forget-me-not came tumbling out as we dragged our companion, now snoring furiously, into the tent feet-first, lest a wandering grizzly deliver a ferocious overnight solution to his relationship train wreck of a life.

We performed this service despite the fact that the philandering fly caster did have an appealing collection of custom rods with him. We had a hunch they would have found their way swiftly into a small mountain of assorted tackle, fly-tying accoutrement, and mounted-fish trophies on the curb for the Monday-morning trash collector, should any unfortunate news arrive from the great green north.

Not all women see fishing as the enemy. But some do, a few to an astonishing depth. The amazing thing is that even some men buy into the paranoia, normally to their grievous regret. Sometimes all one can do is step back and, as if in slow motion, watch the train wreck unfold.

A middle-age man's forever-pledged marriage was in its last painful gasps. From several years of masochistic counseling emerged his wife's seething animus toward my friend's summertime habit of going straight from work to a local trout stream, where he spent most evenings. She claimed his absence had contributed to her sense of alienation. Her response was to sleep with her dentist. With the able guidance of a series of three marriage therapists (the $200 per weekly sessions paid for by hubby), the pitiable man was successfully persuaded to blame himself and his selfishness for their breakup—in his next relationship, he vowed, he would be more sensitive. Meanwhile, his estranged wife was encamped in their house. He continued paying the mortgage while sleeping on a cot in his brother's basement surrounded by jars of pickled beans and cases of Spam stacked neatly on industrial racks, presumably as a hedge against the Apocalypse. Or maybe for snacks the next time the Vikings reached the Super Bowl.

One day the fax machine in my office rang and the picture of an attractive woman began inching through (this obviously dates the story). The telephone rang. What did I think? he asked with the eagerness of a beagle. "She looks like a babe," I replied. "Go for it." Unfortunately, he did. I had failed to fully appreciate the subterranean vise-grip hold of his punitive evangelical upbringing; he wasn't one to flout his supernatural beliefs. When I said go for it, I was suggesting some much-needed cathartic physical intimacy. When he heard "go for it," he heard wedding bells. He hadn't yet filed for divorce.

Why waste time getting to know each other? The compulsion to say "I do" and postpone the surprises until later reaches beyond rigid catechism or common sense. A woman told me nostalgic tales about halcyon days as a little girl fishing with her father on the Big Hole River in Montana. I invited her to the Cape Cod National Seashore to fly fish for striped bass. She wouldn't get out of bed before dawn as success with stripers dictates. Nor would she go swimming in the transparent, sandy shallows after noon because, she feared, something might bite her. "You aren't going to marry me, are you?" she said with a mixture of resignation and anger in her voice. "You know, when I met my first two husbands, I knew instantly that we would get married." Despite being an otherwise bright individual, as underscored by a Harvard MBA, the irony evidently escaped her.

My conscious is clear. Preceding my misinterpreted encouragement to my trout-loving friend to risk diving head-first into another marriage were many, many hours of the usual soul-searching discussion that rides strapped to a one-man pontoon boat relationship headed over the falls. I distinctly recall suggesting that he wait, say, five years before remarrying. "Give yourself time," I advised. "You're a nice guy. There are tens of thousands of smart, single women our age in St. Paul. And by now the smart ones have figured out that the guys they went for 20 years ago are idiots. They would love to meet a considerate guy like you." I even recommended a cozy downtown bar where he should park himself with a soda water and lime (he didn't drink alcohol) where throngs of female executive and agency types frolic at week's end. Just sit there and read a book, I told him. "You do that every Friday afternoon for a month and I guarantee you'll be beating them off with your Sage 4-weight. Make sure the book is right-side up."

I would have done better advising Tony Soprano to turn over his .45 to the nearest traffic cop.

It was the cliché rebound romance. She was toxic. He couldn't see it. With this guy's notions about sex and guilt, he was emotionally wobbly prey without cover. Evidently, exploration of sexual compatibility was permitted only so long as the activity was conducted with at least one eye firmly fixed on the sacramental goal posts while practicing the prescribed mantra: "…till death do we part." To veer from this dogma guarantees a heapin' helpin' of self-loathing and an E-Z pass to Satan's place. There is no inoculation against organized religion's contempt for the Human experience. If God really is watching, he's rolling in the aisles.

During the coming weeks, as the details of my friend's new female love interest emerged, imaginary fire alarms started going off, building to a shrieking crescendo. Call her Candi. She was the daughter of an abusive, alcoholic—and mostly absent—father. Her youthful looks must have stopped traffic. On her 17th birthday she drove out of an automobile dealer's parking lot at the wheel of a shiny new Porsche, a thoughtful gift from a married gentleman in his forties who was the heir to a regional chain of tire stores. A number of sugar daddies later, she attached herself to a ne'er-do-well pretty boy with a cushy job at his mother's tanning salon and a taste for Bolivian marching powder. Together they had an out-of-wedlock child. Then they had another. Candi's best friend, Jennifer, was dating a married outfielder with the Minnesota Twins; she resourcefully supported her lifestyle with several credit cards kept current by a lawyer she had dated previously, and who had more than a passing interest in keeping this bit of personal history from his wife. Etc., etc., etc.

By the time this world-savvy woman happened upon my forlorn friend, time had begun taking its inevitable toll on her chief assets. She was clever enough to notice the competition: a whole new generation of younger, hotter talent fast bearing down in her rearview mirror. The father of her children lost his source of easy cash and had himself become abusive. She told my friend her tale of hard luck—selectively. Life had been hard on her. Now she was ready to make a fresh start. She had lots of ideas for starting her own business. Life had always been a struggle for her. What she needed was time to "find herself."

The man in her crosshairs was decent and hardworking. He made a steady income. Candi told him they were soulmates. She introduced him to a dyed-blue foot-tall chick drink of tequila over chipped ice spiked with an umbrella. He puked in my bathroom.

He set her up in a new apartment by the freeway. Then he started picking up her utility bills, cell phone, and health insurance. Next he signed on the loan for the new car she persuaded him she needed. (She had an interesting posse of creditors chasing her, the most ludicrous from the hospital where she had given birth to one of her sons 10 years earlier.) While her new keeper diligently toiled at his craft day and night, she sunned herself and watched Dr. Phil. She told him she was concerned he was stressing himself out by working too hard—he should tell his demanding clients to lighten up. He took out an uncharacteristic loan on a massive engagement ring.

"You should pay attention to the way Brad treats a woman," she advised me testily. "You might learn something."

Candi screamed and yelled when he told her he was going on a fishing trip we had planned before she entered the picture. Each night after dinner, he dutifully walked a dusty mile and talked to her for an hour from the only pay phone in the area. When he got home 10 days later, waiting for him was a telephone bill roughly equaling the cost of the trip.

He bought a new home. She moved in. The candle incident should have warned him of the impassable reef ahead. Following a brief civil knot-tying ceremony, the new mother-in-law's boyfriend employed a candle on the buffet table to set his napkin aflame. Somehow the slacks of his polyester leisure suit caught fire. The spontaneous scary flare-up was successfully doused on the patio. One disregards such prescient omens, notably anything involving actual flames, at one's peril.

They argued about money. Shouting matches on the front lawn with Candi's deadbeat ex-husband followed. Her kids took to engaging in toilet-paper fights, throwing rolls at the walls and windows. They gathered up the trailing mess and filled the toilets, which when flushed flooded the bathrooms. One day the eldest smart aleck informed his mother's new husband that he couldn't wait until they left for the weekend. He was eager to invite his hooligan friends over for a beer bash/blow-job party. He was 12.

"She had the kid gather up all the photos of the two of us in Mexico and run them through the shredder," he admitted morosely to a friend and me months later, when honeymoon had predictably morphed into hurricane. Funny she hadn't thought to run the $800 bracelet you bought her in Cancún through the shredder, we told him.

Her parting shot was to storm out in a rage and show up theatrically on Valentine's Day with her brother at the wheel of a U-Haul. They backed the truck into my friend's driveway and then ransacked the house for everything she deemed hers, including half the potted plants. "She made sure she took all the best ones," he said.

The last time I checked, my friend was still making monthly payments on the $16,000 ring. He was, however, back fishing again. The sound of Coulee water gurgling gently over rocks and the wind rippling streamside birches offer enduring solace.

\* \* \*

IF THE INGREDIENTS FOR IMPENDING disaster weren't apparent to my fly-fishing friend, he's not alone. Perhaps the reason my antennae were on high alert was because I had been there myself. There were frightening parallels. Today my memory pushes rewind on these travails like an instant replay of a nightmare.

It was nearly 30 years ago. She, too, was seductively attractive (objective observers remarked she could have been a model if someone in the profession had spotted her in her teens). She, too, had two high-maintenance kids. She, too, was allergic to work. She, too, saw my fishing as stealing time and attention away from her. And I, too, was warned.

It's no use. Call it the Good Witch of the North rule. As Dorothy watches the wonderful Wizard of Oz drifting away in his hot-air balloon and expresses dismay that she'll never get back to Kansas, Glinda informs Dorothy that the ruby red slippers she was wearing have all along had the power to take her there. "Why didn't you tell me?" Dorothy asks. "Because you wouldn't have believed me. You had to find out for yourself."

She had big hair. She grew up in a quasi-hillbilly household in the mountains of rural Pennsylvania. The yard had more cars that didn't run than cars that did. They heated their home with a woodstove. There was a bathtub but no shower. She was the prettiest in the family and was convinced her mother was jealous of her. The mother was a piece of work. She sat around in curlers, smoking endless butts, refilling a souvenir-decal cup from the Mr. Coffee machine on the counter, and reading the *National Enquirer*. When her daughters began menstruating and bloodied the sheets, she marched them into the cold cellar, made them strip, and turned a garden hose on them. This was not a nice person.

I directed the publicity for a well-attended conference on acid rain and Atlantic salmon. The personal secretary to the Chairman of Philip Morris in Manhattan called me and invited me to fish with him in Canada at his lodge called Runnymeade. My wife didn't want me to go. She ran around the house slamming doors. I went anyway. I drove home all night in my three-speed International

Scout from the Restigouche River in New Brunswick with a long Styrofoam cooler containing two gorgeous 12-pound chrome-bright fish packed in crushed ice. They ate size 4 Silver Rats I tied with authentic gray fox guard hairs and French silver tinsel, faithful to the original recipe.

We set off from Massachusetts to Pennsylvania for a family reunion. My wife told her mother we were bringing the main course. It was a surprise, she said, but was certain everyone would like it. We stopped at phone booths and called several times from the road to keep her folks updated on our progress. We arrived at 6 p.m. on an August evening. My new mother-in-law informed us that they had tired of waiting for us and cooked burgers and hot dogs an hour ago. There was potato salad and some other leftovers if we were hungry. The grill was still hot so I added fresh coals and baked one of the precious wild salmon in aluminum foil with sweet onions in its belly. I gave my mother-in-law the first plate. The steaming flesh was pink and succulent. My mother-in-law tasted it and remarked, as if surprised: "Hmmm. This is good. Just like that red salmon we get in cans."

We moved to Oregon because I wanted to catch summer steelhead. A penniless fly-fishing bum named Brian (now a world-class fishing photographer) who lived in a shack in Bend told me the little sawmill town in the Cascades was the perfect place because it was just about half way between the North Umpqua and the lower Deschutes. Brian had matinee-idol good looks and commanded the undivided attention of the waitresses at Steamboat Inn whenever he walked in.

In this high-desert ski community we had difficulty making financial ends meet. I was a journeyman magazine editor. She refused to work. We argued about money. Her plans to launch a naughty nightie company called COFFEE TEA OR ME fizzled. Reluctantly, my wife took a job as a part-time cocktail waitress at the Inn of the Seventh Mountain. I watched her kids. She came home late, reeking of cigarette smoke. One night a streaker startled her by dashing naked in front of our Ford Bronco as she was leaving work. Salivating men constantly gave her their business cards, which lay scattered on the nightstand beside our brass bed like dog tags from dead soldiers. Her best friend Irene also worked in the bar. Irene was a single mother who had just been through a tumultuous divorce. She entertained herself every Friday night by making an appearance at my associate editor's unfurnished apartment with a bottle of Jim Beam and a quart of ginger ale and playing a game she called Ride the Pony. My wife announced she was going to a party next weekend with Irene. "Okay," I said. "Where?" "Palm Springs," she said. "We know this guy who has his own plane." Shortly after the party I came home one afternoon to find Irene and my wife on the deck of our cedar home on the way to the slopes on Mount Bachelor. The ladies were well into the wine coolers, fashionable at the time. A pile of empty shotgun shells of my favorite low-base Winchester AA 7½ grouse loads lay on the deck. Back in New England I had taught my wife to shoot. She was a pretty good shot. The training had evidently come in handy as Irene and she took turns working their way through my 33 LP record collection. The vinyl disks must have made good Frisbees. "You're the most boring man I've ever met," said my inebriated wife. "And your music sucks." She had taken decisive action. No longer would she be irritated by the tidewater vocals of Jimmy Buffet on *A1A*, the piano chords of *Mood Indigo* by Duke Ellington, Fleetwood Mac's *Rumours*, *Kinda Blue* by Miles Davis, Graham Nash's *Songs for Beginners*, and the especially despised *James Taylor*, his first but little-known collection of work released on The Beatles' Apple label;

I confessed to having spun "Carolina in My Mind" on the turntable perhaps more than I should. The pieces are likely still in the rabbit brush and sagebrush under the Ponderosa pines.

It didn't help matters that I had spent the night at the apartment of a woman who did graphic-design work for the magazine.

Scene at the kitchen table:

Him: There's no reason to be stupid about this.

Her: Yeah, that's just the way you'd like it, isn't it?

Him: Oh, come on.

Her: No, you come on! You're a real asshole. You know that? *A real fucking asshole.* You think you're *so* great.

Him: That's ridiculous. Let's not make this any worse than it is. We have to deal with it as adults.

Her: Oh, is that right?

Him: You're going to need money....

Her: I'll tell you one thing—the *next* guy is going to have money. I'm sick of this shit.

Him: Look, you're going to need a car. Be realistic— for once in your life. You'll have to get a real job and you'll have to get yourself to work. If we go down to Robertson's now we can get a loan; they'll never give you one by yourself.

Her: Oh, is that right?

Him: Hey, there's no reason to be that way.

Her: Fuck you!

Him: Let's be civilized about this. You're getting hysterical. You need to calm down.

Her: *Civilized?* You're ruining my life and you want me to be civilized? That's so like you. Everything has to be so logical, so planned. Everything's just wonderful as long as *you* get to do what *you* want. Isn't that right? Mr. Wonderful. You're nothing but a selfish jerk. You didn't have to spend $500 on that trip to the Deschutes last September.

Him: It was $600 and I caught a 14-pounder.

Her: Everything is a big joke with you. Prick. You can go to hell.

Him: This instant or can I get in one more steelhead season?

Her: FUCK YOU AND YOUR FUCKING FISHING!

Him: Then fuck you, too. Bitch.


When she started breaking my mother's Norritaké china—stamped MADE IN OCCUPIED JAPAN and which my uncle in the Navy had shipped home to her for her wedding in 1950 and which in my youth we brought out and put away carefully at Thanksgiving and Easter—I came unglued. I had all night staring at the ceiling of cell No. 5 in Deschutes County municipal jail to contemplate the smoldering ruins of my life. *You idiot. You goddamned fucking idiot.* I was scared. I was angry. I was embarrassed and ashamed. I was 30.

I needn't have bothered trying to reason with her over something as inconsequential as how she would get to the job she didn't want. One week later an insurance salesman who belonged to our Trout Unlimited chapter heard about our separation and zeroed right in, the proverbial moth to the flame. He generously gave my wife his Chevy Blazer. Fools rush in. What he told his wife about how the vehicle had vanished, I never learned.

When I was confident she wasn't home, I disobeyed the restraining order and collected a few essential belongings—my fly rods and reels, my 12-gauge over/under and cork duck decoys, my sleeping bag and river duffels, my framed print from a fine watercolor by Chet Reneson called "Tea Time," my family photo album, an armload of signed and first-edition books. I stood there in a daze. Then I remembered the Confederate $20 note a retired fly-fishing banker in the mountains of North Carolina had given me when he had learned

I was a Civil War buff. I felt like an intruder in my own home.

I had no idea where I was going. I drove around aimlessly for a couple of hours and pulled in when I saw a sign that said AVAILABLE. There were tumbleweeds blowing across the parking lot and an overflowing trash bin next to a dull, rusting Dodge Dart without tires dry-docked on cinder blocks. "We have several rooms open," said the heavyset woman at the front desk. "Your pick." I told her I'd take No. 14, my birthday. Nobody had taken that away yet. I placed four hundred-dollar bills on the counter for my first month's rent and another $400 cash deposit against possible damages, and opened the door to a dark room smelling pungently of disinfectant with an orange shag carpet where the previous occupant had parked his Harley each night and from time to time changed the oil.

The only thing worth recalling about this dismal honeycomb of cheap apartments was the 35-year-old divorcee directly upstairs. One evening in the community Jacuzzi, I passed her a gin-and-tonic in a clear plastic cup. Her name was Becky. She wasn't flashy. She was an understated, willowy redhead with bright hazel eyes, a country girl out of the Cheryl Tiegs mold. She had an elegant freckled neck and long, slim legs. She shaved her legs each day and showered twice daily, a habit she told me her mother had taught her. She smelled of baby powder. God, she was lovely. She had two live-in daughters and a cowboy ex-husband somewhere down around Chiloquin, where I knew the well-known bachelor fly tier, Polly Rosborough, lived in a doublewide wallpapered with posters of pin-up girls.

Becky and I discovered a much better use for the shag carpet. "Don't you ever stop?" she asked dreamily. "I have a lot of pent-up energy," I explained. When I came back from Alaska she introduced me to her new lover, the tennis pro at Sunriver. Although I went into temporary mourning, I sensed that I had dodged a serious bullet. I suppose I should have inquired what his favorite bourbon was and had a bottle couriered over, but the sentiment quickly passed.

When Sal, a colleague who worked for Trout Unlimited with me, came to Bend to visit, I invited him to sleep on my sofa. By then I had upgraded to a mattress. He informed me he had an unusual request. I might find the subject sensitive. He'd understand if I objected.

"Fire away," I said.

"I was thinking about inviting your ex-wife on a date," he said.

"She's not my ex-wife yet," I replied.

"Well, she's going to be."

"Are you out of your mind?"

"I've always thought about fucking her. We all have."

Suddenly the overwhelming perversity of the situation hit me. I laughed. "Sure, go ahead," I said, rolling my eyes. "Just don't bring her back here. Give her my regards."

She unleashed three lawyers on me. The first dumped her when he didn't get paid. The second become unreachable when his wife discovered them holding an unscheduled afternoon attorney-client conference at the Best Western Entrada Motor Inn on Century Drive. The third told her essentially what the first two had: He's a working stiff, lady. He has no money. You're trying to get blood out of a stone. Get the blood, she ordered.

One day my lawyer called. "I finally have some good news," he said. "Apparently she has a new boyfriend and she's moving to Portland." I felt the air go out of me in a slow exhale of relief. "You can move back into the house." I listened in stunned silence. I almost couldn't believe what I was hearing. Months had elapsed. She had refused to pay her half of the $650 monthly mortgage payment, even though she had been presented with a court order telling her to do so. So as not to lose the house, I had borrowed money from friends and relatives to keep the bank from nosing in. Plus my own legal bills kept coming.

"When?" I asked.

"She should be gone by the end of today."

Good-bye shag carpet!

\* \* \*

I WAS BACK ENSCONCED IN MY OWN HOME on the hill to celebrate a modest Thanksgiving. Winter passed. She wouldn't sign the divorce papers. My lawyer attempted to schedule a court date. She ignored our entreaties. It got to the point where her own lawyer admitted he was having difficulty communicating with her. I had to do something. It was April. We went ahead and scheduled a court date for late May.

One day I went into my garage and looked over at the pile of boxes and debris she had left. I noticed it when I returned home but hadn't thought much about it. I had planned to clean it all out when warm weather came and the snow melted. I went over to the pile and started pawing through cardboard until I found four or five large black trash bags. They were filled. I opened them and spent the next couple of hours in archeologist mode, sifting through discarded cookie and cereal boxes, cardboard rolls from bathroom tissue, unopened electric bills, more of my mother's broken china, copies of *Glamour* and *People*, stained junk mail, and bouquets of shriveled flowers. She hadn't paid her trash-collection bill, I surmised, so they stopped coming. The trash had piled up all summer. *Interesting*. I continued my mini excavation. I looked more closely at the flowers. There will little note cards attached: "Great meeting you at the party. Let's get together for dinner. Larry" ... "I so enjoyed meeting your girls last weekend. They are darling. Sincerely, Bill" ... "I can't tell you how much our time together has meant to me. I hope we can get to know each other better. Mark."

All the trash bags were empty. Everything of possible use was spread out on the concrete floor. I walked around looking down at the junk. I stooped like a chimpanzee and touched the individual items as if they were curious artifacts. I turned my attention to the paper objects, examining the return addresses, especially anything written by hand—birthday cards, plain envelopes, postcards, etc. Several appeared to match; they were from the same address in Portland. She had refused to tell me where she had moved last November, and her lawyer was under no obligation to tell us. It was worth a shot. I called my lawyer.

"I think I know where she's living," I told him. We discussed what good the knowledge of her whereabouts—if I was guessing right—would do us. I reminded my lawyer that her reason for not agreeing to sign the decree is because it would grant me the house, despite my offer of a 50-50 sharing of appreciation. (The modest down payment had been 100 percent my money.) Her lawyer told the court I left her and her children destitute.

"I'm sure she's being supported by some sugar daddy," I said. "She's not over there eating cat food. He probably makes three, four times what I make. Why don't we subpoena him—drag him into this?"

"Ummm. It's risky. You don't know for certain that's where she is."

"Well, is it legal? Am I within my rights as a citizen to subpoena another citizen, I mean, in a case such as this?"

"If he's in possession of material evidence that's relevant, yes."

"What if it's not him?"

"Then he could either ignore your subpoena, or you might hear from him and you could agree to withdraw it. Or he could cause trouble for you."

"Just what I need. I have to do something to break this impasse. I'll get back to you."

I dialed information: "Multnomah County Library, please." I hung up momentarily and dialed that number. "Would you kindly help me find a telephone number?"

"Just a minute, please, while I transfer you."

"How may I help you?"

"Yes, I'm calling from over in Bend, and I'm looking for something called a reverse directory."

"What address do you have?" I gave her the address.

"Which number do you want?"

"What do you mean?"

"There are two, one for the residence and one for the business."

"Ah, go ahead and give me both."

"The first number is 503.... And the number for Integrated Waste Disposal Systems is 503...."

"What was the name on that residence, again?" I held my breath. "She hadn't given it to me. Maybe she would forget she hadn't.

"Mr. John Doe."

"Oh, yes, that's right. Thank you so much. You've been most helpful."

*Integrated Waste Disposal Systems?* Either she had someone available all hours of the night to replace a leaky gasket in the kitchen sink or she was now "connected." *Yikes.*

It was Thursday. Monday was Memorial Day. The court was supposed to hear Pero v. Pero at 10 a.m. Tuesday. I was out of time. I had one day. In order for the subpoena to have any effect, it would have to be delivered Friday. And he would have to be home. He might have already left for a long weekend. He might not even be her boyfriend.... I busied myself during the weekend tying flies, sustaining myself on large bowls of decadent chocolate ice cream and single-malt scotch.

At five minutes past 8 on Tuesday morning my telephone rang. It was my lawyer. "Bingo," he said. "I just heard from her lawyer. She's ready to sign."

"Amazing," was all I could think to say. I felt myself hyperventilating.

"Just out of curiosity, what did you list on the subpoena?"

"I sent two. They both requested he appear in court today with his tax records for the last three years."

That evening I pulled my gun case out from under the bed. I turned the keys in the lock. I put together the pieces of my over/under methodically, turned the brass handle, opened the glass door, and walked slowly out onto my deck. The sky was a spectacular wash of orange and blue against a backdrop of ragged lavender peaks. Overhead, nighthawks careened and croaked sharply. Standing next to the Weber grill, I surveyed the openings through the thick pine branches. I inserted one shell in the modified chamber, snapped the gun shut, and left it aloft with my left hand. I curled my right hand back toward my chest and, in quick a sweeping motion away from my body, opened my fingers to let the discus fly. I felt the heel of the shotgun buck against my right shoulder and watched the discus disintegrate in a puff of black. It sounded weird, like crumpling Saran wrap. I think the record was *Some Girls*.

\* \* \*

A FRIEND FROM THE EAST COAST CAME OUT to go fishing. We planned to camp on the North Umpqua. We celebrated our reunion at the Ore House, a local watering hole. Three or four laughing young women were sitting at a table filled with glasses. One leaned over. She couldn't help hear we were talking fishing. "Where do you go fishing around here?" she asked with a smile. The situation looked promising.

"We're planning to hit the irrigation canals," I said. "This is first-class canal territory. It's fantastic. We cast right out of the pickup—never have to put down your beer—although my friend visiting from Boston prefers casting saddleback from a llama."

"No! You're joking. *Rilly?* No!"

She was giggly but cute: short-cropped black hair with a wide forehead, button nose and brown eyes. She said they were from Lake Oswego. She and her friends were here for the weekend. She told me she recently met a gal at a party who had just moved to the Portland area: "I think she was married to some guy over here who worked for a fishing magazine. She said his name was Tom somebody. I guess he was a real jerk. Ever hear of him?"

My face flushed red. My throat went dry. I rose from my chair, took her hand gently, bowed slightly and said, "I'm Tom Pero—delighted to meet you. Perhaps you're acquainted with my grandmother, Lizzie Borden."

I didn't know where that came from—yes, I do.

I was born in Fall River, Massachusetts, scene of the notorious murder of the century, nearly 100 years before O. J. On a stifling-hot August morning in 1892, the bodies of wealthy cotton-spinning mill owner Andrew Borden and his wife Abby were discovered hacked to death in their home on Second Avenue. Days before the murders, the humorless Borden, pillar of the community, had ordered his spinster daughter's pet pigeons decapitated because he thought intruders had been after the birds in the barn behind the house. Lizzie attempted to purchase poison at the local pharmacy but was denied. A bloody axe was discovered in the cellar, along with a freshly scoured axe head with a broken handle. Days after the bodies were removed from the house, a neighbor spied Lizzie burning a dress, which she explained was stained with paint and of no consequence. She said she had killed no one. The retiring Christian Sunday-school teacher hired the ethical antecedents to Johnny Cochran, including a former governor of the commonwealth. A sensational 10-day trail captured screaming headlines nationwide. In a rehearsal to the shrunken glove stunt 99 years later, during the trial one of the prosecutors placed a folded dress on the table in front of the judge, pulling it open to reveal the fleshed skulls of the victims. Lizzie fainted. After an hour of deliberation, the jury acquitted her. Bridget the Irish maid—scrubbing windows at the time of the gruesome murders and the only other person other than Lizzie in the house—never said anything that would implicate the accused, even though Lizzie had contradicted herself repeatedly. After the trial, Bridget found herself on a steamship back to the land of the leprechauns. Five weeks later, Lizzie and her sister Emma upgraded their digs to a fine Victorian home on The Hill, a fashionable residential area of Fall River. Pepérè La Croix—my maternal grandfather who would spend a workingman's life skillfully framing houses and calling quahogs "piss clams" and rooting for the Brooklyn Dodgers—and his younger brother weren't about to pass up this opportunity for mischief. The youngsters stood on French Street looking up at Lizzie's shuttered window and recited the singsong rhyme the whole country knew by heart:

Lizzie Borden took an axe

Gave her mother forty whacks

When she saw what she had done

She gave her mother forty-one

But I digress. Back in the Ore House in the summer of 1986, my surprise introduction to the young lady in focus brought the boozy, flirtatious atmosphere to a stone-sober thud. She stared back blankly. "Her boyfriend made her move out of his house, you know," she said. I kept my mouth shut. She smiled faintly. "I guess I, like, said the wrong thing."

"Not at all," I assured her as I turned away and resumed my description of how a steelhead turns on a dry fly.

\* \* \*

YEARS WENT BY. STEVE TELEPHONED FROM Islamorada, Florida. "Tom Pero?" a man's voice asked.

"Yes, speaking," I said.

"This is going to be a strange conversation," he said.

I smiled and looked into my steaming mug of coffee sitting on my desk. Outside the pines were heavy with powdery, glistening snow.

"I've had a few," I said. "Shoot."

"I'm married to Debra."

To me, this was like saying Elvis—there was no need for elaboration.

"Oh," I said, as much a question as a statement.

"Do you know where I'm calling from?" he asked.

"Yeah," I said. "You're in the Keys. I've never been there but I know where you live. It's famous for saltwater fishing."

I was immediately on guard. After listening to him for five minutes or so, however, I realized that there was nothing contrived. He was authentic. Steve was an oil-rig engineer. He was away from home for a month, then home for a month, then away. His travels took him all over the world wherever there was oil drilling, from the Gulf of Mexico to the North Sea to Singapore. He had met my ex-wife at a bar (by now, where else?) in Beaverton, just outside Portland. He had married her six months ago.

"She told me a lot of bad stuff about you," he said. "But something inside told me to call."

"I'm sure she painted me every shade of scarlet complete with pointed tail and horns," I said. "I'll tell you exactly what I told her: I'm willing to accept 50 percent of the responsibility for the fiasco that our marriage became. But she was never willing to accept any."

"That's not why I'm calling," he said.

"What can I do for you, then?"

"I need your advice."

"Are you serious?"

"I'm afraid I am. You obviously know her—probably better than I do. She's run away from me. She took all my credit cards. I don't know what to do. I still love her."

"Well, I sure as hell can't tell you what to do. I'm not exactly the ideal source of advice for a relationship in distress...."

I didn't make it to Islamorada ("village of islands") for 15 years. I had all but forgotten about the phone call when, pulling into the 30-foot mermaid ringed in lights at the Lor-e-li, in a flash I remembered in that *this* is where she ended up, at least temporarily. At the dock there is a sign atop a pole in the water that says, I'LL GET YOU A FISH IF IT TAKES YOUR LAST DIME. I couldn't help wondering what on Earth she must have thought of this place, a glorified mangrove swamp that fancies itself the Sport Fishing Capital of the World. Tarpon and bonefish iconography is everywhere you turn There are billboards showing men wielding fly rods. At restaurants and at gas stations—more than in Roscoe or West Yellowstone or Jackson Hole, more than in any other fishing town in America—males hiding behind designer Polaroid sunglasses in turquoise and pink and blue fishing shirts with little Velcro tabs mill about, the fly-fishing version of the flying monkeys. She couldn't escape it. She had driven 3,421 miles only to confront the inescapable: she could run but she couldn't hide. This wasn't the Pink Palace on St. Pete Beach.

Maybe I should have taken him up on his offer. We might have made a congenial day of it. After some initial discomfort, we could have stopped at the Trading Post for pastrami on rye to feed the tame tarpon at Robbie's Marina; then onto happy hour for Key lime martinis at the Zane Grey Angler's Lounge at World Wide Sportsman; ordering spicy tuna rolls at Kaiyo; finally, in a scene right out of one of local resident (and avid fly fisher) Carl Hiaasen's raucous novels, we could have compared notes between shows of fleshy adult entertainment at Woody's.

* * *

WHY ARE MEN OBLIVIOUS? DID WE LEARN it by watching too many reruns of the Three Stooges? Is it a gender-specific allergy that percolates over a lifetime from food we are fed as infants, but to which females are immune? Or is it a characteristic hardwired into our DNA, reaching back to our days trading jibes with cave bears or joining in on leisure activities aboard the original Viking cruise ships?

A friend of mine telephoned home during a late-lunch afternoon between the noontime Hendrickson hatch and the evening spinnerfall on the Beaverkill. After polite chit-chat he asked, "Would you please put Cynthia on?" To which his mother-in-law replied, "She's not here."

"When do you expect her back?"

"I don't. She gave me instructions to clean out the house."

Three hundred and fifty miles away, my friend on the other end of the line was speechless.

"She never told me why she was marrying you and she hasn't told me why she's leaving."

Do we fertilize our unwitting obtrusiveness by slurping down a dozen oysters on the half shell? (Slice up a ripe lemon with your finest eight-inch chef's knife and anoint mine liberally with all the juice and a hint of Tabasco sauce.)

As Michelle—a vivacious blonde I once mistakenly believed was the love of my life—said upon learning I had been evicted from one of those "self-awareness" and "personal-growth" weekend for which she had hopefully signed me up, "You just don't get it, do you?" The $400 fee was non-refundable. No, I didn't, but there was magic in the air that July evening when she and I hiked into the misty pool where she caught her first steelhead on a fly, and then—15 minutes later—a second. Now that's my idea of self-help.

\* \* \*

ROD RAGE HAPPENS. NO GENDER IS EXEMPT. Once the ex-husband of a woman I was dating entered my hotel room without my knowledge or permission, opened the long aluminum rod tubes (this was in the old two-piece days) pulled the rods still in their sacks out part way, and splintered them just above the cork handles.

The insurance adjuster was puzzled. I shrugged my shoulders and speculated that the destruction must have happened "in transit," which, in a way, it did.

There's a story about Jack Hemingway that's worth retelling.

"I can still see him standing there," 78-year-old Frank Moore told me, pointing to an old-fashioned crank telephone, its pair of black bells worn shiny. The dark wooden box once hung at Steamboat Inn; now it adorned the wall of Moore's hand-hewn log home overlooking Oregon's rushing North Umpqua. "Right away I knew something was wrong." In July 1961 Jack had come in from a Sunday morning immersed in fly fishing for summer-run steelhead, one of the things about life he loved most. He held the phone to his ear to learn the horrible news that his famous father, writer Ernest Hemingway, had shot himself.

"If there was a river he was going to be on it," Moore said about his friend Jack. "He'd go out before daylight and come back after dark." Moore recalled one night when Jack stayed out on the river, sleeping on rocks at a prime holding pool called Station, so come dawn he'd have undisputed first crack at the fish. And Jack's wife, Puck, was left to see that Jack's mother, Hadley, and her husband, Paul Mowrer, who were visiting with them at Steamboat, were kept entertained. When Hemingway finally appeared at the cabin, barely in time for dinner, Puck had whipped herself into a lather. She blurted out, "For two bits I'd break your goddamned rod!" So Jack took out a quarter and threw it on the bed. She ran over, grabbed the Silaflex Medallion fiberglass rod Jack had been casting, and smashed it over her knee: "There—what do you think about that?"

"I don't mind," replied Hemingway, "but Frank's gonna be mad as hell when he finds out you broke his best rod."

* * *

HOWEVER YOU SLICE IT, IT'S AN UNEASY truce. Fishing is a greedy mistress. Fishing takes time. And money. This tension lurks, in the words of the immortal song-writing team of Richard Rogers and Lorenz Hart, at the heart of "the classic battle of a him and her." Either the bathroom gets a new designer sink or you are in seat 8A on a LAN Chile flight to Argentina for some dry-fly fishing in February. Survival tip: Don't plan your trip for Valentine's week.

When one is afflicted with the unshakable fever of fly fishing, there aren't many escape routes. You and yours can become conspiratorial fishing bums in arms, perhaps as locally recognizable as one of those cute poster couples, wading happily ever after into the mayfly-dancing sunset, with his-and-her fishing vests and matching back casts. In some over-the-top fishing relationships, one partner becomes the enabler. Almost always the instigator is male. You know the type: He's a part-time guide in summer, sleeping in his pickup. When the snow flies he's a denizen of consumer fishing shows or a fly-tying recluse, when he's not trying to snag a free trip to Belize or Chile. Meantime, she's a full-time nurse, office administrator, veterinarian, sales manager, bookkeeper—fill in the blank. Hey, someone has to pay the cable TV bill. Or you can agree to disagree and go your separate ways: *I'll play golf or tennis, ride a horse, jump on a jet-ski, hit the designer outlets, read Danielle Steele by the pool, get a peppermint body wrap and almond-oil rub-down by Raul; you go stand in the river looking silly.*

Alternatively, there's cash. While he's preoccupied with identifying invisible bugs squirming in the surface of the Henry's Fork in Idaho, one or two no-limit Platinum cards can come in handy at Nordstrom.

Back in the go-go days of the 1980s, when Donald Trump's hair actually was red and he frequented the ornate corridors of The Plaza Hotel—a leggy model a foot taller than The Donald invariably fixed on each arm—I found myself sitting at an impeccably set table in the Grand Ballroom. The occasion of my presence was a gathering of anglers to help raise money to perpetuate wild rivers and their wild salmon.

I rose to introduce myself to a handsome couple. In my altar-boy days I would have assumed they were father and daughter. She was about my age. She was a stunning brunette with high, porcelain-smooth cheeks and exotically sculpted eyebrows. Preparing for her entrance must have taken hours of make-up time. After a suitable interlude, my teeth feeling the cold ache of the ice cubes I had been self-consciously crunching, my eyes surreptitiously migrated down her curvaceous black-stockinged form, settling momentarily on a pair of wicked-looking stiletto heels, above which was conspicuously anchored a diamond-encrusted Lady Rolex.

I thought I had peeked with the utmost discretion. Not a chance. She shot me a superior, nose-up Mona Lisa smile. I was instantly reminded of the hilarious folly of any attempt to pull the wool over several million years of sexual evolution, and that the old adage about being able to take the boy out of the country but never the country out of the boy applies with equal authority to altar boys and confessionals. This girl's best friend definitely wasn't a Bogdan reel.

In the long run, shoveling cash at the relationship often creates as many problems as it masks. One never quite knows if it's your dash and élan she's after or the glee of never having to sleep on anything less than 400-count Ralph Lauren designer 100 percent Egyptian cotton that has the happy couple in rapt gaze.

A Southern gentleman of the old school inherited the family plantation and looked forward to spending his life more or less on permanent safari. He married his high school sweetheart, who ran off with one of his quail-shooting buddies. He killed so many birds with his worn Parker double that by age 35 he had shot his ears out. Half deaf, he decided to take up saltwater fly fishing, and moved to Key West. After a respectable period of sulking, he resumed his roving eye for the ladies. One he had his eye on was a former *Vogue* model. She was estranged from baseball god Ted Williams. (The retired Red Sox slugger and she had met over the Pacific when he passed her a note. He was returning from New Zealand. "Who's asking?" her return note said. "Mr. Williams. A Fisherman," he wrote. Fifty million Sears catalogs notwithstanding, she had no idea who he was. Just because the last man to hit .400 in the majors turned out to be a foul-mouthed, moody lout was no reason for her to stay off the water. She had been brought up in Vermont and enjoyed the outdoors.) Ever ready to rise to the occasion, the smooth-talking southern gentleman took to providing complimentary guiding whenever she was in the mood for a little fishing. When she hooked a tarpon she removed the top of her bikini to fight the rampaging silver king. Competing guide boats took to carrying binoculars.

On Duvall Street a lively young waitress in white short-shorts caught his attention. He forgot about Miss South Carolina (runner-up) back home—a gorgeous, educated blonde whom he had left in charge of his Cadillac. He also suffered a bout of temporary amnesia about the brunette vixen's six-year-old kid. He asked her to marry him during the Chicken Fest parade as the "Coop de Grâce" float was passing by. One day in May while he was staked out for tarpon in the Marquesas, she disappeared without leaving so much as a note. He arrived home that evening to a house that looked as if Sherman had stopped by on his march to the sea.

He selected his next wife from a carefully orchestrated series of interviews with young women at the University of South Carolina. In response to the advertisement, she told him sure, she could adjust to traveling the world and being pampered. What she didn't tell him was that one of her boyfriends was serving time and another was in the process of becoming a she. For the better part of a decade they fished more exotic places than any other couple on the planet—sailfish in Costa Rica, steelhead in British Columbia, marlin in Cuba, dorado in Brazil, tarpon in Africa, salmon in Norway, permit in Mexico, and on and on. They both racked up many world records on the fly.

He grew older. She grew restless. She wanted more culture in her life—opera, for instance. He put her through real-estate school and set her up with the best firm in town. She hit the market just as it was heating up. She sold a mansion on the bay at Big Pine Key to a former heavy-metal guitarist with Mötley Crüe. "Who?" he asked. She moved out and filed for divorce. She hasn't picked up a fly rod since.

"I taught her everything," he moaned, sitting on his poling platform on the Hell's Bay skiff during a 72-hour lull in the action. "I hadn't planned on starting from scratch one more time, but I guess that's what I'll have to do. The first one left me for my best friend. The second one left me for that gynecologist...." *And your last one left you for Don Giovani.*

"Bobby," I said, looking aft from the foredeck with 12-weight line draped over my bare sunburned feet like limp yellow spaghetti. "You've lived one hell of an exciting life."

"Yes I have, Tommy," he said with a smile. "Yes I have."

The last time I saw him he was preparing his 6,000-square-foot hacienda for a comely Columbia University medical student freshly arrived from Slovenia, less than half his age and pining for a green card. Seducing a seven-inch marble trout is a far cry from slugging it out with a seven-foot striped marlin, but smart girls learn quickly.

\* \* \*

IT'S NOT ALWAYS THE WOMEN WHO LEAVE the men over an addiction to fishing. On a June morning at daybreak I met an elegant old man wearing an ascot. He was sitting in the sand with his easel, waiting for water spouts, for the sky to do something interesting. He told me he had been painting watercolors on this beach since 1962, and over the years had caught many cruising bonefish here.

"I had six children; I didn't like children," he said. "I had a house; I didn't like houses. I had a lawn and I didn't like lawns. And I hated snow."

So one day Millard left his well-paying position in the art department at Hugh Hefner's sizzling magazine in Chicago, closed the driver's door in his car, and hit the gas to the farthest, warmest place he could find. He phoned his wife, Jane, and told her he was in the Florida Keys—that he wasn't coming back. He said she would hear from his lawyer about a divorce.

"What will it take to keep our marriage together?" she asked.

"You probably wouldn't like it here," he said.

"Try me," she said.

"And," the artist told me, "Jane and I were together for 40 more years.

\* \* \*

AMONG THE MOST PUZZLING FLY FISHERS I've encountered are the female groupies to whom publicized prowess with a fly rod appears to serve up some sort of aphrodisiac. Considering the normal state of goofy impoverishment of most males delusional enough to spend most of our waking hours pondering endlessly what fake foods a pea-brained fish might be enticed into ingesting—or, worse, trying to eek out a subsistence living at the sport—one wonders why any woman wouldn't back away slowly, hoping it's not contagious.

The joker who launched the myth that psychobabes make great lovers should have his tongue impaled with a 3/0 Woolly Bugger and dangled at daybreak from the railroad trestle over the upper Delaware at Hancock.

Call her Sandra Shrewsbury. She called herself the Girl from Texas and handed out business cards with her first name spelled out in a lariat. She said she was a photographer. She said she had developed a keen interest in making portraits of famous anglers. She suggested a meeting to show me her portfolio. The meeting lasted at most an hour; nothing improper happened or was suggested. The next day I opened my mailbox to find a hand-tinted notecard featuring a picture of the Girl from Texas standing on the hood of a 1955 Studebaker. He was wearing red cowboy boots and tipping her Stetson. That's it. He had titled it the "Auto Erotic" series. Her accompanying personal note to me read, "Let me be your hood ornament."

What I wasn't aware of at the time was that I wasn't her first target. The Girl from Texas had recently pursued one of my editors-at-large, a well-known steelheader living on the Grand Ronde River in eastern Oregon. She met him at a fishing clinic in Seattle, professing great personal admiration for him and his contributions to the sport. He made the mistake of accepting an invitation to have dinner at her place. Upon returning home, several hundred miles away, Shrewsbury began telephoning him relentlessly. She foresaw great things in their creative collaboration, she told him; they were soulmates. My friend didn't think so, and told her so. She kept calling. When John—in all the years I had known him a gentle, soft-spoken, extremely patient man—couldn't take any more, he insisted she please stop. She screamed at him, "You're ruining my life!" The next week a Valentine's card arrived in his mailbox with the photo of a bleeding heart impaled on a picket fence.

When things didn't work out with either of us, the Girl from Texas moved on to Bill, a ferry ride across Puget Sound on the Olympic Peninsula. Now she had expanded her repertoire—now she was an accomplished professional photographer *and* an outdoor writer. Her "assignment"? A series of articles about steelhead guides. Bill was a full-time steelhead guide. Unsuspecting, Bill took the bait, providing Shrewsbury with complimentary river trips and introducing her to the owner of a cabin along the Sol Duc River, which Shrewsbury talked the owner into allowing her to house sit at no charge for the spring fishing season.

Bill was an experienced steelhead fly fisher whose guiding was highly valued. He was paid several hundred dollars a day for his services. Steelhead season is short. He was almost always booked. Yet Shrewsbury demanded more free fishing trips. Soon the now-familiar cycle of relentless phone calls and answering-machine messages began; Bill's wife intercepted many. When Bill wouldn't play along, she grew angry with him, and began a campaign of rumor and innuendo to discredit him among fellow guides on the peninsula as well as neighboring townsfolk. She sent a rambling, scandalous letter to Bill, in which she accused him of lying about his commitment to conservation and "… a lack of honesty and respect for women." She shamelessly accused him of leading a sordid personal life and of not sharing "… your knowledge with me as promised."

One final horror waited, however, when Bill tried to retrieve the spey rod he had loaned the Girl from Texas in happier times. After repeated but unanswered requests the she return the fly rod, he drove to her cabin, saw his rod in her dilapidated

Jeep (which, ironically and predictably, Bill had given her), reached in the open window and took back his fishing tackle—without ever touching her. Shrewsbury, who had come to calling herself "The Sol Duc Spey Princess," began screeching at Bill, kicking and scratching him. Then telephoned the Clallum County Sheriff's Office in Forks to shrilly report she was being assaulted.

Fortunately for Bill, the real victim, his stalwart wife was present as a witness to the fact that nothing of the sort had happened. When the responding deputy sheriff grasped the farce, he spoke with The Princess for an hour to try to calm her down and convince her that, under the circumstances, it probably wouldn't be a wise idea to file assault charges. The volatile situation appeared defused. Later, Shrewsbury called the public prosecutor's office in Port Angeles, threatening to file charges against the deputy sheriff!

And, you may be wondering, how did I survive to tell the tale of this sordid little psycho-drama? At one point I wondered if I would. Never was my anxiety higher when one otherwise delightful spring day when The Girl from Hell appeared unannounced in my driveway. When I asked her to leave she glared at me through narrowed dark eyes and pursed lips and half whispered, "Don't make me hurt you," throwing her car in reserve and tearing up a corner of my front yard as she sped away.

On the heels of Shrewsbury's trying to get me thrown out of the Outdoor Writers Association of America on ethics charges and attempting to stir up a hornet's nest by writing to and telephoning investors in my magazine, I received an official-sounding letter from a young lawyer stating he represented Shrewsbury. He alleged that, by publishing pictures taken by his client without proper remuneration, my magazine had broken federal copyright laws carrying minimum penalties of $37,500,000 (you're reading the zeros correctly). Would the magazine—for publishing photos worth a market value of maybe $500—please forward a check to the tune of $17,147.34 within 10 days?

Resisting the impulse to ask if they preferred cash or check, we hired our own lawyer, a bone fide copyright specialist, who provided evidence of canceled checks bearing Ms. Shrewsbury's signature and explained to her lawyer that no copyright violation had occurred: the magazine and Pero had acted in good faith. No response. Seven months later the same lawyer sent me another long letter threatening legal action. We responded in a professional manner that they had demonstrated nothing new. Next her lawyer telephoned me directly and told me I was in big trouble. I told him that I took a dim view of extortion. If he really thought they had a legitimate case, I suggested, he should probably go ahead and sue us. We never heard from him again.

We did, alas, hear from Shrewsbury, true to form, many months later, when a notice inviting me to small claims court was served to me at my office. Same assertion: I had published her pictures with permission and without compensation. On the morning scheduled for hearing, when I appeared at the clerk's window to ask for directions, the clerk looked at me in a peculiar way. (I later learned that Shrewsbury had been stalking the court for weeks, sitting in on small claims hearings that didn't concern her and pestering the clerk about which judge would be assigned her case. They evidently smelled trouble.)

Shrewsbury v. Pero was, as I recall, one of 16 or 17 small claims hearings scheduled to be heard that day. They ran the gamut of banality from clumsy eviction of non-paying renters to mysteriously missing lawn mowers. This was a first for me; when I momentarily forgot what an utter waste of my time this was, I found the King County District Court gathering rather campy.

The presiding judge began by calling roll. A dozen or so names in, she called "Sandra Shrewsbury?" No response. And again: "Sandra Shrewsbury?" Still not in the room. In her introductory remarks, the judge explained that 15 minutes had been allocated for each hearing; we should each respect the clock and each other's time. The judge next recited the order in which the various small claims would be heard by the court. All would be in this room, she explained—all, that is, but Shrewsbury v. Pero. That trial would be in the adjoining courtroom across the hall and presided over by another judge, the Honorable so-and-so.

*What?* My mind was racing. *What the hell is this about?*

Into the next courtroom I wandered, took my seat, and waited. And waited. Ten minutes after the hearing was supposed to begin, a visibly agitated Judge so-and-so sarcastically welcomed The Girl from Texas as she bustled into the room with a disheveled armload of papers, magazines and various stuff: "Nice of you to make it, Ms. Shrewsbury." Whereupon the plaintiff proceeded to demand a change of venue—in other words, another judge.

When his Honor asked why, she said she could not trust him to preside impartially.

*Holy shit!* I remember thinking. *This would be like the designated hitter taking his sweet time stepping into the batter's box, and then turning around and asking the umpire to trade places with the first-base umpire because the batter doesn't trust his strike zone.* I could barely suppress my glee. This might be fun after all.

One hour and forty-eight minutes later (I kept track) after the judge had demonstrated time and time again an excruciating degree of patience ("I'm trying to help you make your point, Ms. Shrewsbury, but you'll have to help yourself by being more than a little clearer about what it is you're saying the defendant did or didn't do that harmed you."). He finally grew weary of Shrewsbury's disorganized, largely incoherent and hostile tirades and announced that the time had come for her to bring her argument to a close. Shrewsbury angrily threw back another sheet of paper on the easel and began furiously scrawling anew with the court-supplied Magic Marker.

"But I'm not finished!" she looked up at him in protest.

Firmly slamming his gavel to the bench, the judge glared down at her and relied, "Oh yes you are. The court finds in favor of the defendant. The court thanks you both for your time. You are free to go."

\* \* \*

THEN THERE WAS THE GIRL NEXT DOOR. I made her acquaintance one soft summer evening at a barbecue block party on our suburban cul de sac. She said she had heard there was a fishing guy living in the neighborhood. She wondered why she hadn't seen me around. I said it's because I had been away. She asked where. When I told her Havana she smiled and said she didn't realize she was living next to Indiana Jones. "Hardly," I replied. Some women prefer the fantasy.

We talked. She appeared a spirited woman. She exuded self-confidence, effervescence. Later that evening, I asked another neighbor what he knew about her. "Fake boobs," he said, washed down by a long gulp of Heineken. Fools rush in. Within days I was mixing chocolate martinis for her and transporting her lawnmower to the repair shop. Within weeks I was teaching her to cast.

Topping the list of reasons to steer clear of the Girl Next Door was her surly 13-year-old son. With time, however, I came to appreciate the practical advantage of this conspicuously flashing red light. Every other weekend she turned over the reins to her ex-husband, who had once done a professional stint as a bodyguard at the Playboy Mansion Beverly Hills, and whose corrupting influence she feared had the impressionable youngster on a fast track to the nearest juvenile detention facility. She tried to instill discipline and respect—or so her version of the parental tug-of-war went—while the ex countered by indulging the kid with every PlayStation video game and digital gadget imaginable, without consequences for his recurring insolence. One of the costs of spending time with the Girl Next Door was listening to her rant on about the pandering and profligate ex. On a positive note, during the intervening 12 days when the son's nose and forehead were glued to the home computer screen, she kept a discreet distance from me.

She would appear at my door Friday night and leave sometime Sunday. I never knew quite what she would come dressed in but, after several sessions, I could probably have done a fairly credible job identifying a good portion of the Victoria's Secret catalog. She left once-worn samples as souvenirs. It was a kind of neighborly fair-trade agreement: I fed her far better than anyone ever had and lit candles for dinner; she played dress-up and pranced in front of orange flames warmly licking the wintry fireplace. She believed that in a previous life she had been a Moorish princess. (*Note to women: What is it with this princess stuff?*) She read thick books on astrological signs and how people matched up. She insisted I walk around and open the car door for her on the way to Costco; when I absentmindedly forgot she became indignant and refused to get in until I got out. She was a gusher of lovey-doviness. "You've been waiting all your life for a Latino girl, haven't you?" she said, pouting lips glistening. "You *lu-u-uve* me, don't you?" Everything was *"mi amoré"* or "honey." She complimented me for knowing just where to find her G-spot. She worked for a plastic surgeon kept busy by strippers, gay male baristas, and idle wives of Bellevue lawyers. When she brought me around to display me to her friends and workmates, I could always count on hearing, "If he cooked like this for me all the time, I'd marry him!" This went on for months.

She didn't like the wet and the cold. *What are you doing living in the northern rain forest?* I wondered.

She asked me to take her somewhere warm. She dreamed of floating in blue-green water, she said. A bonefish guide in the Caribbean owed me a favor. I sent money to reserve a cozy beachside house for a week on Andros Island. For Christmas I gave her a pair of Patagonia Marlwalkers and a ticket on Bahamasair. She gave me a pair of Orvis bonefish Wonderlines, the boxes cheerily signed to me personally by the line's designer. (I'm still impressed she made that connection.) I gave her hyper kid a locking-blade titanium pocketknife with a note advising him not to kill himself.

Later that winter we enjoyed a pleasant week of snorkeling, fishing and exploring the tropical island. She was intrigued by the large orange sea stars and held them up for me to photograph. When I wasn't broiling lobster or grouper we ate fresh conch salad every night at a cozy conch shack owned by a colorful character named Sly Fox. The breezes were warm, the Kaliks were cold, the rum tasty. The Girl Next Door, a gymnast in her youth, was quite athletic and had become a remarkably capable beginning fly caster for having had all of a couple of quick half-hour lessons aiming at paper plates scattered on her backyard lawn. On our way back through Miami, we stopped for a romantic evening at Mosaico, one of my favorite restaurants.

Once home in the gray chill of the Seattle suburbs, things were quiet for several days. When the Girl Next Door made her next Friday appearance, I welcomed her to a table set with tulips in her favorite color. A fragrant fire crackled in the background. I poured her a crisp Willamette Valley pinot gris, then busied myself grating the parmesan into a crisp Caesar salad while keeping an eye on a succulent piece of bright orange spring chinook salmon simmering in a savory court bouillon. But after dinner, instead of making her saucy spawning run up the stairs to her customary come-hither position under the king down comforter, she paced briskly out the front door, pausing briefly.

"I've decided," she said, glancing over her shoulder with a flip of her shoulder-length chestnut curls, "that you're a better neighbor than lover. But I'll still help you clean out your garage." I heard her humming as she walked away.

Her exit was indelible. It was one of those clock-stopping, did-I-just-hear-what-I-thought-I-heard? moments—an instant classic for the relationship portfolio. True to gender, I was momentarily discombobulated. Her deftly executed emotional hit-

and-run had blindsided me. Mugged between the sofa and the coat closet, I was left alone to ponder the startling news of my inadequacy between the sheets, coinciding with the successful completion of her mission to the blue-green water. Charming. At least I'd have a tidy garage. Days later she appeared genuinely baffled at my lack of enthusiasm for her suggestion that I come over and look at pictures from our trip. The absurdity was sublime. This was one self-absorbed *chica*. In the end, as Woody Allen said, all you can do is laugh.

She followed up by forwarding an Internet joke, the gist of which was that two retired Floridians—Jacob, age 92, and Barbara, age 89—walk into a pharmacy. They run down a list of products they're looking for: walkers, wheelchairs, medication for everything from rheumatism to arthritis, and Viagra. The pharmacist assures the elderly couple he carries it all. "Good," says Jacob, "we'd like to use this store as our bridal registry."

Hi Tom:

This e-mail made me laugh, but this will never be you. You won't need a bridal registry while you're off exploring continents, slaying wild game, and fishing the waters blue and green. Have a good day. GND

\* \* \*

AGE HAS AN ASSUAGING EFFECT ON A younger man's conflicting makeup of outward swagger and clumsy insecurity, the vulnerable paradox that young females rely on. Most pimply adolescent males are no match. Faced with the requirement of sustaining a level of coherent communication in order to obtain sex, the testosterone-driven youth is dumbstruck. Most are in a panic. *If she says no, will there ever be another?* Over time, the answer eventually dawns on us: yes—in fact, if we floss and gargle regularly, keep boorish thoughts to ourselves, and remember to show up in public, a steady supply of willing women can be counted on to parade through one's life.

In the meantime, we proceed to recklessly run our lives through the emotional Cuisinart of our own diabolical design, squandering precious fishing time as if there were an infinite supply of weeks and years ahead on the water. Some become suicide bombers in drift boats.

At a sportsmen's show I met a promising young man who dreamed obsessively of earning his living by spending days on the river. He soon rocketed his way to prominence as one of the best fly-fishing guides in Wyoming, commanding $200, then $300, then $400 a day, plus tips and complimentary Christmas deliveries of gourmet Omaha steaks. He was booked solid. He was turning away prospective paying clients. A fellow guide stumbled across him rolling in the sand under the cottonwoods with a female client, their waders around their ankles. He lost his home. His wife took their child and moved back to New Jersey. The last time I glanced at the wreckage he was selling his rods on e-Bay and working for $10 an hour cleaning swimming pools in Denver.

Some rabid anglers surrender without a whimper, blithely signing on for a lifetime of domestic indentured servitude, Thoreau's famous "quiet desperation" outcome—*I used to fish, when I had time.*

An old classmate and I celebrated his first Skykomish steelhead with a rich Honduran El Rey del Mundo Robusto Larga, and his first Abaco bonefish with a tasty Cuban Upmann Sir Winston. He reacted to the visitation of mid-life crisis by accepting an invitation for a mid-day tryst from one of the checkout clerks at the large store he managed. He roared up on his Harley, having instinctively begun making preparations for the mid-life crisis one year earlier with the hog's procurement. As they were tearing off each other's clothes with their teeth, the hotel room started rolling like a dingy in 30-foot swells—it was the Nisqually earthquake, at magnitude 6.8, the most violent in the Pacific Northwest in 40 years. They jumped back into their clothes and made a mad crawl to the elevator. (I guess this is one way to make the earth move.)

There's an amusing aside to this story. When they eventually consummated the sticky deed, the man's wife discovered his hanky panky from an e-mail on their home computer: "Oh, baby, I just love your new porn site!!!" He was a secret dirty surfer. The wife confronted her Harley-hugging husband by asking gravely where he was making these re-volting movies. "Did he tell you in your garage after the kids were in bed?" I asked her facetiously when the aggrieved woman shared the story days later in a remarkably self-effacing manner as she stood in my front yard of gloriously blooming spring laven-der ringed in white roses.

The girlfriend popped the question to her sur-prised husband over breakfast: Would you kindly move out of your own home? The store manager moved in, trading one wife and three kids for some-one else's wife and three kids. His ex-spouse is an excellent Italian cook; his new significant other is an excellent Italian cook. (Forget the sexual politics—I would have happily refereed a time-out for the chance to taste-test a duel over best-of-lovers' risotto and veal scaloppini with Parma ham, anchovies, capers and grappa.) The Harley sits parked in his new garage, in no immediate danger of losing value due to excessive mileage. His fly rods remain snuggly in their cases. The fish are safe.

Others keep casting and somehow manage to survive the relationship gauntlet until the balance of power gradually shifts. The 16-year-old cheerleader who once held all the cards and whom we mistook for Aphrodite is now saddled with two ingrate kids demanding chauffer service to the mall and soccer practice. Our erstwhile goddess of love and beauty has taken refuge in pints of Chunky Monkey, and is worried about whether the man in line with her at Starbucks notices her. (No, I don't. I'm daydreaming about making a perfect presentation with one of Dustin Huff's secret crab pattern to permit tails flashing in the Yucatán sunshine.)

"You're a better neighbor..." Instead of a younger man's pit-of-the-stomach emotional flinch at the Girl Next Door's inelegant *adieu*— the best romance-chilling up-yours I had ever heard—I was overcome with an airy feeling of elation: more wonderment than abandonment. To this very moment I can't explain it. What could I say? All I could do was stand in the doorway and marvel at the eternal promise of feminine caprice—ultimately unknowable—and, like Sinatra's circumspect "Man in the Looking Glass," smile.

"Your call," I said as *mi amoré* disappeared into the night, having learned a long time ago that it always is. I guessed I would be fishing alone for a while.

### Note on the Author

Thomas R. Pero of Bothell, Washington, was Trout Unlimited's first full-time editor of *Trout* from 1977 to 1993, twice winning Conservation Magazine of the Year from the Natural Resources Council of America. He served as founding editor of *Wild Steelhead & Atlantic Salmon* and *Fly & Fly* magazines.